JAYA FLAVA

JAYA FLAVA

*A celebration of food,
flavour and recipes
from Sri Lanka*

Tasha Marikkar

HARPER DESIGN
An Imprint of HarperCollins Publishers

First published in India by Harper Design 2024
An imprint of HarperCollins *Publishers* India
4th Floor, Tower A, Building No. 10, DLF Cyber City,
DLF Phase II, Gurugram, Haryana – 122002
www.harpercollins.co.in

2 4 6 8 10 9 7 5 3 1

Copyright © Tasha Marikkar 2024

P-ISBN: 978-93-5699-624-3
E-ISBN: 978-93-5699-755-4

The views and opinions expressed in this book are the
author's own and the facts are as reported by her,
and the publishers are not in any way liable for the same.

Tasha Marikkar asserts the moral right
to be identified as the author of this work.

All rights reserved. No part of this publication may be reproduced,
stored in a retrieval system, or transmitted, in any form or by any means,
electronic, mechanical, photocopying, recording or otherwise,
without the prior permission of the publishers.

Written and illustrated by Tasha Marikkar
Photography by Malaka Mp (www.malakamp.com),
Design consultant: L.L. Manura Pathmila Alwis, **Additional layout
work:** Fold Media Collective, **Food styling**: Anishka Fernando and Tasha
Marikkar, **Crockery and cutlery**: Dankotuwa, **Additional photography**:
Anushka Wijesinha, Ryan and Jonathan Wijeratne

Printed and bound at
Manipal Technologies Limited

To my mother Neela, my father Zarook, my sister Leah, my best friend Venya. Without your generosity, love and unwavering cheerleading of me, this book would have never been born.

White House, Kalkudah

Contents

Wait, What's Jayaflava?

Jayaflava is a celebration of everything Sri Lankan; its past, its present, its idiosyncrasies, its ability to be endearing and infuriating at the same time, its incredible resilience. To me, this island is always at odds–how its inhabitants are the most brilliant, warm-natured people who are also the most frightening, life-threatening drivers on the road. But I love to celebrate everything about it, even its not-so-great bits.

Sri Lanka is both multi-ethnic and multicultural; full of wonderful traditions and religions that have made an indelible mark on the people and its food. The best way to describe a Sri Lankan's nature simply is that all-knowing, non-meaning headshake. If you know Sri Lanka well, you'll know it means neither yes nor no, 'maybe I did what was asked', or 'maybe I didn't', or 'what to do?'. To me, this gesture is the ultimate 'Sri Lankanism'.

We've had tough times, but what shines through is how Sri Lankans will rally together when other people are without–they will take you into their homes, give you the little they have, share their meals with you, until you are back on your feet. I've witnessed this incredible feat a few times in my life–during the war, the innumerable floods, the Easter attacks, the 2022 peaceful protests and most famously during the tsunami. What brings me joy is how sharing meals is ingrained in our culture; no meal is individual–it belongs to the collective. That in itself has taught me many life lessons. Food truly unites the people of this island and portrays its incredible ethnic diversity.

But what does Jayaflava actually mean? A hybrid of the words 'Jayawewa' and 'Flava', I coined the term to celebrate my two homes, Colombo and London. Jayawewa, which means celebration and victory, is most famously used by Sri Lankan politicians or protestors to mobilize and inspire their masses. Flava, one of my most favourite early noughties Brit terms (largely inspired by Craig David), seemed to be the best way to encapsulate the dynamism, style and freshness of Sri Lankan cuisine and to describe me as well. My mother often refers to me as an achcharu (more of that later), alluding to the fact that I am a mix of different ethnicities: Sinhalese, Ceylon Moor and Colombo Chetty. This has given me a truly unique view on the country and exposed me to many cultural traditions. In my family, Christmas was just as celebrated as Ramadan and I have been blessed to eat all the amazing dishes that are cooked during these celebrations, many of which are featured in this book.

My hope is Jayaflava *will spark a Sri Lankan food revolution, where people will learn to cook authentic Sri Lankan dishes and help make our food a home-cooked staple around the world.*

My Food Credentials

'If Yan can cook, so can you' was one of my earliest food memories. I was an 'indoor' child who spent countless hours in front of the television. Daytime TV was my jam, and growing up in Sri Lanka we had the choice of only four (yes, four!) TV channels—two state-owned and two private. The private channels would always broadcast cooking shows. Watching Martin Yan smiling into the camera while using a gigantic cleaver in the early afternoon taught me my cooking fundamentals. After the show, I would try to cook one of the dishes I had seen that day, or attempt to bake a sweet treat from one of the countless cookbooks that we had at home. I started cooking when I was six and this became a big part of my personality; I am a self-confessed feeder.

One of my fondest memories growing up as a child was family meals. My maternal grandparents insisted that we spend every Sunday eating lunch at their house. This was where my wider family got together and I started to learn the principles of how to pair Sri Lankan dishes. Family meals on my father's side was a further education in eating culture—my relatives were very specific on the styles of meals that they would cook; but ingrained into my mind were big extended family meals, sitting on woven leaf mats, eating biryani out of huge sawans (serving bowls) and sharing this meal with another four to five guests.

When I was younger, I had no interest in cooking Sri Lankan food. Instead, I focused on learning European dishes. It was only at university in London that I started to miss Sri Lankan food—its punchy, spicy flavours were lacking in my meals, and I found myself carrying a bottle of tabasco in my bag to counter the bland cafeteria food. My desire to eat better inspired me to cook the food of my childhood. To be a better cook overall, I took short courses where I could—at Leiths and Le Cordon Bleu—and this helped me cook curries with more flair. I really upped my Sri Lankan culinary game when I started living with my flatmate and best friend, Venya Wijegoonewardene in London. Her constant craving for Sri Lankan food helped improve my skills in cooking island dishes, and I added to my repertoire of Lankan food. I even reached out to my wonderful network of aunties who taught me their secret recipes.

Sri Lanka is deeply diverse and beautiful, and these traits translate into its food. This book is a homage to this ethnically varied island. I have attempted to ensure that every community which has a few recipes that are unique to them is represented in this book.

I hope that through the course of cooking with this book, you will find an insight into the culture and wonderful heritage of Sri Lanka!

Multicultural Sri Lanka

How Sri Lanka's multiple ethnicities have shaped its food and its heritage.

Sinhalese

The ethnic majority of Sri Lanka, the origins of the Sinhalese can be traced back to the Indo-Aryan settlers who intermarried with the native island tribes. The Sinhalese are predominantly Buddhist, with a significant Christian population—a reflection of the island's colonial past. Reading the works of Knox and other early writers, one can trace how traditional Sinhalese food has such fantastic everyday vegetarian dishes, and a few but utterly perfect fish and meat dishes usually reserved for special occasions or guests. This resonates with Buddhist philosophy where meat is discouraged but not explicitly prohibited. Among the Sinhalese Christians, meat is more abundant. Christmas dishes in particular have delicious relishes of South Asian ingredients like ghee, nutmeg and cloves paired with festive foods like yellow rice.

Since most Sinhalese were farmers, they were thrifty in their food habits. Meals were simple yet delicious, with one or two vegetable curries and a sambol, allowing them to stretch their harvests for longer periods. This also probably spurred the development of many traditional Sinhalese recipes involving pickling, sun drying, smoking, 'jaadying', etc, and the hundred ingenious ways of using rice, from main dishes to desserts. Through the years the Sinhalese have acquired a reputation as good bread makers among other ethnicities—particularly the Tamil and Muslim communities in the North and East—who adore 'Sinhala paan'.

Main festivals: Sinhalese and Tamil New Year, Vesak, Poson poya, Christmas

Ceylon Tamils

This ethnic group has a long history stretching back to the Jaffna Kingdom and the associated Vanniyar chieftaincies. Most Ceylon Tamils are Hindus, though there is also a significant Christian population within the community. In Lankan–Tamil food culture one can view a course of evolution that stays true to their history on this island, but it also incorporates later influences from the colonizing Westerners, and the more modern internationally inspired flavours. Lankan–Tamil desserts have close similarities to their Sinhalese counterparts, with ingredients like jaggery, rice flour, coconut and sesame seeds, apart from the gingelly oil, which is distinctive of Tamil cuisine. Everyday food is usually rice and curry, with their recipes often comprising garden ingredients like hibiscus, pumpkin, moringa sticks, aubergine and okra. The fiery orange Ceylon Tamil crab curries dotted with dark green moringa leaves are so legendary that there are restaurants in Colombo built solely on their reputation for making authentic 'Jaffna crab curry'. The palmyra palm wine is another iconic element that I love about this food culture. In fact, all palmyra-based, foods from snacks, savouries, sweets and porridge to drinks, form a significant part of Ceylon Tamil cuisine. This is because the palmyra palm (Borassus flabelliformis) is an important symbol of the Ceylon Tamils' cultural capital Jaffna, to which most still have a strong connection.

Main festivals: Sinhalese and Tamil New Year, Thai Pongal

Indian Tamils

The majority of 'Indian Tamils' are immigrants who arrived in Sri Lanka from southern India to serve as the labour force in the colonists' tea, rubber and coffee plantations. There are also many other smaller groups of trader and merchant communities like Sindhis, Bohras, Memons, Nadars, Malayalis, Gujaratis, Bharathas and Baluchis (often called Afghans) who first migrated to Sri Lanka from the Indian peninsula, sometimes even as far back as six hundred years ago.

The ingenuity with which the migrant communities have built a version of their homeland's food culture from their sparse plantation housing gardens; the profoundness of the connection that Sindhis establish between nourishing the mind and the body—their bhajans always being followed by community dining; the absolute gastronomic delight of beloved Bohra treats like samosas, godamba roti and Bombay sweets—these are just a few of the many, many Indian Tamil culinary elements that I find to be incredibly important to the diversity of Sri Lankan cuisine.

Main festivals: Sinhalese and Tamil New Year, Thai Pongal, and Diwali

Ceylon Moors

Also known as Sri Lankan Muslims, this ethnic group is a mix of Arab merchants and Islamic immigrants from India. The influence that they've had on the evolution of Lankan cuisine is remarkable. From the halwas that inspired the local sweet aluwa, the colourful glasses of saruwath lining roadside booths—a direct descendant of the Arabian sharbat—the insanely sweet local candyfloss bombai-motai, the food-coma-inducing biryani and the most popular Sri Lankan street food of all time—kotthu (thought to have been invented by Batticaloa Muslims to make use of leftovers) are all Moorish influences that have changed Lankan cuisine forever. I must mention what is probably the queen of desserts in Sri Lanka, which happens to be a Moorish pudding—watalappan. I think everything that needs to be said about watalappan is summed up in this quote by JP De Fonseka, published in the *Times of Ceylon*, 1937; 'The Muslim's is a sweet tooth. He has a pudding, (for which Allah be praised) called wattialiappam, a soft succulent one of jaggery and eggs and all the spices on earth, which goes down with a demure sweetness like that of the hour is in paradise'. Even today in Sri Lanka, Muslims are known for their delicious food, and Moor restaurants proudly display signs that read 'Muslim kadē' (Muslim shop) that have become a guarantee for terrific taste.

Main festivals: Ramadan and Hajj

Burghers

'Kāla, bīla, joli karana minissu' (people who eat, drink and make merry) is a common phrase with which other Sri Lankan ethnicities fondly identify the Burghers. In fact, Robert Percival (1805), visiting Ceylon shortly after the British took over the island, observed that the Burghers began their day with tobacco and gin, and ended their day with gin and tobacco. The word 'Burgher', mainly referring to the Eurasian descendants of the colonizing Hollanders, derives from the Dutch term 'burg', meaning city, to simply indicate 'citizen'. However, all Burghers are not necessarily of Dutch origin, as the VOC (Dutch East India Company) employed people from other neighbouring European countries as well, particularly France and Belgium. Later, they intermarried with Eurasian women of Portuguese origin, which explains the enormous influence that the Portuguese Creole language had on the Burghers. They are a community with a rich culinary tradition that uses Dutch fare and borrows Lusitanian and even British practices with an interesting interplay of Sinhalese and Tamil cuisine. Even today, the centre of this community—The Dutch Burgher Union in Colombo—is a local favourite for their legendary love cake (originally known as Bolo d' Amor before the English name gained popularity), lamprais and the homemade ginger beer that is still made by 'aunties' in Burgher households.

Main festival: Christmas

Colombo Chetties

Although a majority of them migrated here during the colonial period, there are enough mentions of 'Situ, Hetti, Setti or Sēthi' in ancient stories, history dating back several centuries and folklore, hinting at just how long this ethnicity has actually been in Sri Lanka. Now known as 'Chetties', this trader community has mixed with mostly Burghers, Indian Tamils and Sinhalese. A popular children's game's rhyme that goes *'athuru, mithuru, dambadiva thuru, rāja kapuru hettiyā'* shows how deeply the Chetties are woven into Sri Lanka's ethnic fabric. Their roots are connected to the Tana Vaisya trading caste in India, and even today, Lankans associate Chetties with good business sense.

The Sri Lankan Chetty sensibility is obvious in their food philosophy, with ideas like 'food is medicine, medicine is food'. Deliciously spiced, thickly curried vegetables and sprouts with little gravy, rice or kurakkan (a heavy, healthy brown flour also known as ragi), fenugreek leaf rotis and long pepper rasam are some of the Chetty classics linked to their original South Indian roots. Later, when the Chetties' business sensibilities led them to embrace Christianity during the Portuguese, Dutch and British rule, their diet incorporated more meats and fascinating interpretations of Western cuisine.

Main festival: Christmas

Malays

'Ja-minissu' (Java people)—as the Sinhalese call them—are known for their easy-going approach to life, and interestingly for being excellent soldiers. Maybe this is connected to their origins as political exiles, chieftains and soldiers brought here from the Indonesian archipelago during the colonial era. *An Account of the Island of Ceylon* by Percival mentions that Malays at the time emulated 'terror and destruction', always carrying their poisoned daggers and krises. Their language, Bahasa Melayu, is a mix of Sinhala, Tamil and Malay, making it a distinctly different dialect.

Malays have brought in some of the characteristic elements of Lankan culture, including the sarong and the paper kites that punctuate our August skies, while their food has merged flawlessly into Sri Lankan cuisine. Malay achcharu (Malay pickle) is easily the most popular, a staple in the traditional Lankan menu next to kiribath and curries. The to-die-for nasi goreng—a mix of spiced fried rice with flavourful meat topped with a sunny-side-up egg—that is probably one of the most popular city foods in Lanka today, has its origins in the Malay fare. Sirikaya, which some say inspired the Moors' watalappan, the cheenakueh cake that the Sinhalese embraced as seenakku and dodol that has become a cottage industry in the Deep South, are all Malay desserts. However, the way I see it, the most important Malay influence on the Lankan cuisine is the sambol—an irreplaceable element of Lankan cuisine that brings together coconut and spices, which eventually inspired the iconic Sri Lankan pol sambol.

Main festivals: Ramadan and Hajj

Veddas

These are a people that have fascinated anthropologists, historians, linguists, and anyone interested in human cultures. Veddas were the last indigenous tribe of Sri Lanka, living immersed in nature in caves, using bows, arrows and daggers to hunt game, wearing bark-cloth, their faith resting on the departed souls of ancestors. Legends trace them to the beginning of Sri Lanka's recorded history, but archaeological and anthropological studies show that Veddas are much older than that, going back to the Stone Age.

Veddas are a real paleo community who lived off hunting and gathering in the jungle. A major part of their diet was wild bee honey, which they also sourced for villagers in exchange for knives, arrowheads or rice. They would know where hives would mature and climb trees while burning dry leaves to ward off the bees. May and June were the peak honey-gathering time, during which they would go on a two-month-long hunt. Veddas were so resourceful that they only took rice and pepper with them on these hunts, because everything else was hunted or gathered. Robert Knox described how Veddas preserved meat, mentioning that a hollow tree cutting would be filled with honey and then with meat before being sealed shut with natural clay. True jungle-dwelling Veddas are no more. But their culinary culture and food habits have been recorded enough for us to trace the earliest beginnings of Sri Lankan cuisine.

Sri Lankan Food: Eating in Full Colour

Growing up I was a terribly fussy eater, often refusing to eat rice and curry. This only changed in adulthood. And when I finally came around to preparing my own Lankan meals, I turned to my mother, Neela, for advice. And she would unfailingly say, 'Your dishes should reflect the colours of the rainbow.' By this she meant, always try to have one vegetable dish that is yellow, another that is green, one that is red (which could be a meat dish) and one that is any other colour you can think of. I do not know if this rings true, but Neela insisted that eating different-coloured dishes ensured that one had a balanced meal.

Sri Lankans approach their meals with a set menu in mind. There are certain curries that go with hoppers (like seeni sambol, pol sambol and a fish curry) and there are ones that definitely do not (like a mallung or a polos curry). For instance, a traditional Sunday lunch in a Sri Lankan household will likely be yellow rice, and as a result, it is common to serve a black chicken curry alongside it. This sounds like a potential minefield so, to help you plan your meals, I have curated a series of meal options under 'Sample Menus (page 38)' for reference.

There are some cooking terms that you may have not come across before, but a majority of Sri Lankan recipes begin with a 'temper'. A temper is a term that we use to describe our version of a starter, like a 'mirepoix' in French cooking or 'soffritto' in Italian cooking. Our temper usually begins with onion, garlic, curry leaves, pandan leaves and/or ginger. To this we add in different spices to formulate the basis of our curries and give them an added lift when we finish others; for example, a temper for a dhal is added only at the end.

In Sri Lanka we share all our meals, so to honour that ethos, all the recipes have been weighed out to serve two to four people. Some of these recipes can be a bit time consuming, but because curry keeps extremely well, developing more flavour in the fridge over a few days, you can cook in bulk, like I do. I always pack my leftovers into plastic containers and either freeze them or refrigerate them so that I have flava-packed lunches or dinners for a few days.

When Getting Started: What Do You Need?

Right off the bat, do not be intimidated by the number of ingredients that go into each recipe. My advice: if you are interested in cooking Sri Lankan food, buy the critical spices and curry powders. Once you've done that, most of these recipes will be quick to cook. The principles of Sri Lankan cooking are quite straightforward so I would urge you to cook using your own measures and weights. Once you are confident about the dishes, dial up the heat, make it more aromatic, or keep things mellow—it is up to you.

Spices and Other Essentials

The spice investment is crucial to your Sri Lankan culinary journey. Ideally, it should include the following: roasted curry powder, unroasted curry powder, cinnamon, coriander seeds, cumin seeds, fennel seeds, mustard seeds, fenugreek seeds, chilli powder, chilli flakes, pepper, turmeric powder, cloves, cardamoms, desiccated coconut, tamarind (fruit or paste) and maldive fish (can be substituted with bonito flakes). It always helps to have stock cubes, cans of coconut milk, a jar of chutney and lime pickle in your cupboard as additional flavour boosters. There is a very rare dried fruit that we use in our cooking—it's called goraka (garcinia quaesita), which is difficult to find outside of Sri Lanka. But, if you do find it, buy some immediately. If goraka is unavailable, tamarind paste makes for a good alternative.

Pots, Pans and Coconut Crockery

You will also require some specialized cooking equipment. The basics you need include the following: large frying pans, a stringhopper press, hopper pans or a mini wok, a steamer, a pestle and mortar, a hand blender, a food processor or a coffee grinder for grinding spices and grains, an electric beater, oven-proof cookware and large heavy-bottomed pans for curry making! Most importantly, a lot of Sri Lankan recipes call for fresh grated coconut and for this, you will need to break open the coconut and at times even extract the milk. You will need a coconut grinder, a cleaver and a blender for it. There is a substitute, which is desiccated coconut soaked in thick tinned coconut milk to hydrate it, but I would always recommend fresh coconut over that.

The 'island cookware' is always available where a Sri Lankan community exists. In 2015, I was shopping in Wembley Central and I was blown away to see that they sold a stringhopper machine that made 200 at a go!

To learn more about the recommended spices, refer to the Spicyclopedia chapter (page 257). Hopefully, when you reach the end of this book, you will no longer be a seasoning padawan but a spice jedi.

unroasted curry powder

Yields **70g** | Time **10 minutes**

INGREDIENTS

10 fresh curry leaves

3 tbsps coriander seeds

2 tbsps cumin seeds

2 tsps fennel seeds

5g cinnamon stick (½ quill)

1 ¼ tsps turmeric powder

1 tsp ginger powder

5 cloves

½ tsp garlic powder

1 tsp dried lemongrass pieces

4 cardamom pods

½ tsp fenugreek seeds

1 tsp mustard seeds

1 tsp salt

METHOD

1. Roast the curry leaves in a small non-stick pan over a high heat for 1 minute until the leaves curl and get a bit brown but retain some of their green colour. Take off the heat and set aside.

2. In a spice grinder, add all the ingredients and grind into a fine powder. Empty the curry powder into an airtight container and store up to a month.

roasted curry powder

Yields **70g** | Time **15 minutes**

INGREDIENTS

3 tbsps coriander seeds

1 tbsp cumin seeds

2 tbsps fennel seeds

1 tsp fenugreek seeds

1 tsp mustard seeds

2 tsps peppercorns

6 whole dried red chillies

2 tsps white rice

5g cinnamon stick (½ quill)

12 fresh curry leaves

1 tsp ginger powder

6 cloves

¼ tsp garlic powder

5 cardamom pods

1 tsp salt

METHOD

1. Take a small non-stick frying pan or wok and bring to temperature over a high heat. Roast the coriander, cumin, fennel, fenugreek, mustard seeds and peppercorns together for 5 minutes. You are likely to hear popping noises. Once they are considerably darker in colour, set aside to cool.

2. Next, over a high heat, roast the whole dried red chillies, the rice and the cinnamon stick together for 2 minutes. The rice and chillies should have blackened on one side. Set aside.

3. Roast the curry leaves for 1 minute over a high heat, until the leaves have curled and are lightly browned but retain some of their green colour.

4. In a grinder, put all the ingredients and grind into a fine powder. It should be very dark in colour. Empty the roasted curry powder into an airtight container and store up to a month.

jaffna curry powder

Yields **70g** | Time **15 minutes**

INGREDIENTS

8 whole dried red chillies

1 tbsp rice

3 tbsps coriander seeds

2 tbsps cumin seeds

1 tsp fenugreek seeds

1 tsp mustard seeds

3 tsps peppercorns

20 fresh curry leaves

½ tsp turmeric powder

1 tbsp white rice

1 tsp ginger powder

1 tsp dried lemongrass pieces

1 tsp salt

METHOD

1. Take a small non-stick frying pan or wok and bring to temperature over a high heat. Roast 2 whole dried red chillies and the rice together for 5 minutes. The rice and chillies should have blackened on one side. Set aside.

2. Toast the coriander, cumin, fenugreek, mustard seeds, and peppercorns together for 3 minutes. They should be golden and aromatic. Set aside to cool.

3. Roast the curry leaves for 30 seconds over a high heat, until the leaves have curled and lightly browned but retain most of their green colour.

4. In a grinder, start by putting all the leftover whole dried chillies and grind the chillies into a rough crumble. Then put all the rest of the ingredients in and grind into a fine powder. It should be red and dark in colour. Decant the Jaffna curry powder into an airtight container and store up to a month.

Coconut: the Lifeline of Sri Lankan Food

The humble coconut is the holy grail of Lankan cooking. We use it in all its forms, in a number of ways. The nutritious coconut water from a mature coconut can be drunk to improve digestive health. This 'first water' is used for fermenting rice when making hoppers and can be used in curries too. Sri Lankans use grated coconut in a number of dishes, most famously in sambols and mallungs. It is used as a flavour enhancer for many meat and seafood curries, added by simply roasting and grinding it into a spice mix. The grated coconut is also utilized for making coconut milk. Water is mixed with the grated coconut, blended and squeezed through a sieve to create the milk. In Sri Lankan custom, three milks are extracted from one coconut. The 'miti kiri' is the first milk, thick and creamy, and is often used to finish off a curry, rather than to start one. The 'devani kiri', which is the second extraction, is often used as the starting milk to cook meat, seafood and vegetable curries, and finally the 'thunveni kiri' which is a very thin coconut milk (mostly water), is often used for vegetable curries and long-cook curries.

Sri Lankans tend to not drink the kurumba (which is green in colour), often used across the world for coconut water, as we know that we can get more from a kurumba than just the water. This is the coconut that matures into the hairy brown coconut that you see in so many stores and supermarkets across Asia. We don't just eat it, we repurpose the husk to scrub pots and pans and use the polished shells to make cooking utensils. For Sri Lankans, the young green coconut is nowhere near as valuable as its older mature self.

Us Lankans love to drink king coconut (aka thambili); bright orange in colour and full of electrolytes, it is a natural saline, perfect for hangovers. Some insider knowledge: simply drink it as a chaser when having an alcoholic beverage and you will feel so much better after a night out. Arrack and thambili is a perfect combination.

A quick tip when buying a mature coconut: shake it. Make sure that you can hear the water swishing inside of it. That is how you will get a good coconut.

JAYAFLAVA
Sample Menus

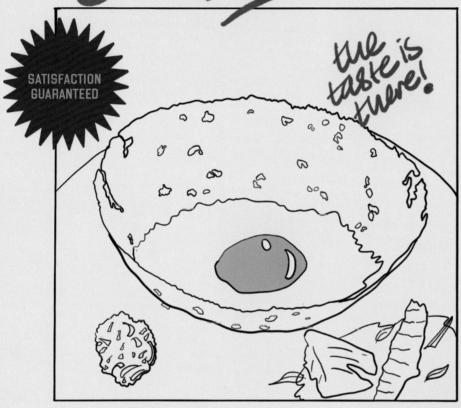

the taste is there!

SATISFACTION GUARANTEED

In Sri Lanka, there is an eating culture that we live by—rotis, gravy-pullers and rice dishes have a set style of curries, sambols and chutneys that we eat them with.

Across this book, the serves often say 'between two to four people'; this may seem confusing at first, but it's simply because Sri Lankans will eat a minimum of four to five curries with every meal, so invariably people will eat less of each curry. However, if you are going to prepare only one or two curries, then one recipe will be enough only for two people and will not stretch for a party of four.

To help first-timers wrap their head around how we pair our meals, I have set out a series of sample menus. There is a whole host of options in each set menu I have designed; however, that does not mean that you have to cook them all. They are suggestions, so pick and choose how many you want to cook in each set. I would recommend one rice, roti or gravy-puller, and then at least three accompanying curries.

Happy cooking!

A TYPICAL
Sunday lunch

Kaha baath	81
Black pork curry/	203/210
Black chicken curry	
Brinjal moju	180
Carrot top sambol	114
Tharaka dhal	175
Ala thel dhala	167
Polos curry	184
Garlic curry	159

HOPPER MEAL

Hoppers	105
Lunu miris	120
Mirisata malu curry	137
Mutton pooriyal	196
Seeni sambol	126

STRINGHOPPER FEASTING

Stringhoppers	109
Pol sambol	118
Egg curry/Omelette curry	206/216
Chicken mulligatawny/	73/155
Prawn curry	
Ala thel dhala	167
Tomato curry	179
Polos curry	184

A BIG RICE AND CURRY LUNCH

White rice	
Jaggery beef curry/	199/209
Red chicken curry	
Thalana batu	177
Moringa mallung	160
Tharaka dhal	175
Fish fry at the beach	56
Bittergourd sambol	128
Tempered beetroot fry	183

BEST FOOD QUAL

ROTI BREAKFAST

Pol roti	85
Tinned fish curry/Prawn curry	138/155
Red chicken curry	209
Lunu miris	120
Tharaka dhal	175
Seeni sambol	126

BIRYANI AND ALL THE TRIMMINGS

Chicken biryani	86
Tharaka dhal	175
Pineapple curry/Raw mango curry	171/133
Mint sambol	120
Malay pickle	122
Banana blossom fry	131
Lamb curd curry	200
Cashew curry	190

GODAMBA ROTI

Godamba roti	89
Black chicken curry/Lamb curd curry	210/200
Prawn curry/Cuttlefish curry	155/151
Pol sambol/Green pol sambol	118/117
Tomato curry	179

A CRAB CURRY

Crab curry	146
White rice/Steamed rice	
Pol sambol/Green pol sambol	118/117
Moringa mallung	160
Ala thel dhala	167
Godamba roti	89

A SEAFOOD FEAST

White rice/Steamed rice

Kooniso curry/Prawn curry/	152/155/
Cuttlefish curry	151
Malu mirista curry/Ambul thiyal	137/148
Moringa mallung	160
Fried okra curry	172
Green pol sambol	117
Raw mango curry	133

KIRIBATH BREKKIE SPICY AND A SWEET OPTION

Kiribath	110
Tinned fish curry/ Malu mirista curry	138/137
Red chicken curry	209
Lunu miris	120
Seeni sambol	126
Pani pol	126

A filling vegan rice and curry

White rice

Tempered beetroot fry	183
Cashew curry	190
Raw mango curry	133
Polos curry	184
Tharaka dhal	175
Carrot top sambol	114
Leek fry	164
Garlic curry	159

THE ULTIMATE SRI LANKAN KIDS' PARTY

Ribbon birthday cake	233
Fish cutlets	47
Chicken curry puffs	61
Prawn patties	63
Devilled eggs	52
Hot butter cuttlefish	59
Cassava chips	64
Fish fry at the beach	56
Chocolate biscuit pudding	234

Short Eats and Bites

An essential part of Sri Lankan snackage is 'bites', better known as short eats. These quick little meals or yum parcels play a central role in the day of a Lankan. Whether it is that 10 a.m. breaktime snack in the school tuck shop, or that much-needed afternoon pick-up at work with tea, or that essential bar snack with your drinks, or a little meal for entertaining guests before dinner... short eats are very important to a Lankan.

It could be argued that they are not very historic meals in our culture—a number of them being inspired by European snacks that were brought to Sri Lanka by colonizers and traders. A patty evolving from an empanada or a mini pasty. The cutlet, a round bite-sized version of a Portuguese croquette. A Chinese roll, although unheard of in China, is a Lankan version of a deep-fried spring roll. The links are endless—but there is nothing quite like a Sri Lankan version of a quick snack.

Lemme Tell You about Shawty

As a child, the school tuck shop was one of the locations instrumental to an education in short eats. As an adult, the local watering hole would be where one would learn about bites. These snacks are integral to Sri Lankan culture.

My fondest memories of short eats are at school—I was a grumpy morning person (still am) and this would be my first real meal of the day. My usual tuck shop purchases would be a Coca-Cola Buddy and a Chinese roll, or a fish patty that would cost about 15 LKR, a major cost back in the days of primary school. But an undisputed school favourite was 'kimbula bunis' (crocodile buns), a hybrid bread roll in a shape resembling a croissant, covered in lots and lots of granulated sugar.

Where to get the best short eat is a hotly debated topic in Sri Lanka; if it is not homemade, then is it Perera & Sons, or Sponge, or Fab, or Klassy? For me, it is Klassy hands down, and I think many would agree. No one likes short eats more than my sister. Typically, no matter what time of day, she (like many Lankans) always has a small siri-siri (plastic) bag of hot short eats sitting on her desk at work—a chicken pie, a bacon-and-egg puff, a few fish patties are the usual suspects.

Bites are another key Sri Lankan snack—and if you are having a beer or an arrack with a mate, your typical bites would have to be anything devilled, some hot butter cuttlefish and, of course, cheese toast. Chatting whilst gorging on bites and booze, with the background music of a calypso band singing 'Welcome to Sri Lanka', makes this an A+ experience.

fish cutlets

Serves **12-14 cutlets** | Time **1 hour** | Ethnic Roots **Portuguese heritage**

INGREDIENTS

For the filling

½ red onion (75g), finely minced

2 tbsps coconut/ neutral oil

2 garlic cloves, finely minced

6 inches of pandan leaves, torn into fairly large pieces

8 curry leaves

100g tinned sardines or mackerel

¼ tsp cinnamon powder

½ tsp turmeric powder

½ tsp chilli powder

½ tsp salt

½ tsp pepper

250g waxy potatoes, peeled, boiled and mashed

juice of 1/2 lime

250ml neutral oil for frying

For the outer coating,
place each item in a separate bowl

150g plain flour

1 medium egg

120g breadcrumbs

Arguably Sri Lanka's most famed short eat, the cutlet is a key recipe to have in your cooking arsenal. You can substitute the tinned fish with minced chicken or beef, but ensure the meat is browned and cooked through before adding in the mashed potato. Make this gluten-free by coating the fish cutlets in gluten-free flour (or cornflour) and with polenta or gluten-free breadcrumbs.

METHOD

1. Warm a frying pan over a medium heat. Fry the onions in 2 tbsps of oil until translucent. Add in the garlic, pandan leaves, curry leaves and cook for 2 minutes.

2. Add in the tinned sardines/mackerel and mix. Next, add in the cinnamon powder, turmeric, chilli powder, salt and pepper and mix well. Add the mashed potatoes and combine well, ensuring that the fish is flaked into the potato. Cook for 3–4 minutes. Take off the heat and finish with the lime juice.

3. Let the fish-potato mixture cool. Remove the pandan leaves and then divide and roll the fish mix into 12 equal-sized balls. Take a ball and roll it in the flour to coat it, ensuring all sides are covered. Next, dip it into the egg wash, then quickly dredge the ball in the breadcrumbs, ensuring an even coating on it. Repeat for the next 11 balls.

4. Take a small deep pan or a hopper pan, fill with frying oil and set it over high heat. Test if the oil is hot by dropping a few breadcrumbs, if it bubbles and turns golden the oil is ready. Add in the cutlets in batches of 4, stirring to make sure that they are evenly cooked. They are finished when they turn golden brown. Eat whilst warm!

kimbula bunis (crocodile buns)

Serves **8** | Prep **1 hour 40 minutes** | Time **20 minutes**

INGREDIENTS

For the dough

10g yeast

30ml milk

1 large egg

30g butter, melted

150ml warm water

400g all-purpose flour

40g sugar

10g salt

50ml condensed milk

For the final step

Egg wash (1 egg and 50ml of water)

150g white sugar

Extra flour for rolling the dough (30g)

METHOD

1. In a jug, mix the yeast, milk, egg, melted butter and water with a fork. Set aside to bloom for 10 minutes.

2. In a stand mixer or a large bowl if mixing by hand, add the flour, sugar and salt. Give it a quick mix by hand. Stream in the condensed milk (pour into a centre well in the flour if mixing by hand). Knead on medium speed in the stand mixer using the dough hook for 5 minutes, or by hand for 3–5 minutes.

3. Pour the yeast-milk solution into the flour and knead on medium speed for 10 minutes or by hand for 10–15 minutes. This should come together as a smooth ball. Remove from the mixer and knead by hand for a few minutes to ensure a smooth and glossy dough.

4. Place in a well-oiled bowl and let it rest for 1 hour or until the dough has doubled in size.

Flour the surface, roll out the dough and then roll into a log, then divide into 8 equal pieces.

5. Roll each piece into a long isosceles triangle, pulling the top of the triangle to make it skinny. From the base, use the tips of your fingers to roll each piece very thinly to make a croissant-like shape finishing with the tip of the triangle. Fold the top of the triangle into the body of the bun so that its merged. Set aside and repeat for the rest of the dough pieces.

6. Next, in a small baking tray, spread the sugar in a thin layer. Take one bun and using a pastry brush, cover the top and sides of the bun with egg wash. Then carefully roll it in loose sugar, ensuring that the tops and sides are well covered. Place on a baking sheet lined with parchment paper. Repeat for the rest of the buns. Ensure that there is space between each bun as they will grow in the oven.

7. Preheat the oven to 180°C. Cook the buns for 15–20 minutes until they are golden brown (depending on your oven the time could vary). Take them out of the oven and allow to cool for 5–10 minutes before serving. Eat plain or with lots of butter.

This is a kid favourite (probably because it is covered in sugar). It was one of my fondest childhood tuck shop meals. You can always substitute the all-purpose (AP) flour with bread flour, and if you run out of egg wash or sugar in step 6, then make or add some more.

devilled chicken

Serves **4** | Prep **15 minutes** | Time **20 minutes**

INGREDIENTS

For the chicken preparation

300g boneless chicken breast/ thigh

½ tsp salt

½ tsp pepper

½ tsp chilli powder

½ tbsp cornflour

2 tbsps oil

For the devilled sauce marinade

3 tbsps Sriracha (hot sauce)

3 tbsps tomato ketchup

1 tbsp fish sauce

1 tbsp tomato paste

2 tbsps soya sauce

10g ginger and 10g garlic blended with ½ tsp sunflower oil

Prepare

4 shallots, quartered

2 banana capsicums, cut diagonally

½ large leek (white), diced diagonally

2 large raw green chillies

3 spring onions, cut diagonally

2 tomatoes, quartered

METHOD

1. Cut the boneless chicken into equal 10cm pieces. Mix the chicken in a bowl with the salt, pepper and chilli powder. Then toss in the cornflour and ensure all the pieces of chicken are properly coated. Heat the oil in a frying pan and then fry the chicken pieces (in batches if necessary) until golden brown. Set aside.

2. In a bowl, mix all the ingredients for the devilled sauce and set aside.

3. In a frying pan, heat a little sunflower oil. Add in the shallots, banana capsicums, diced leeks, green chillies and spring onions. Sauté for 3–4 minutes or until the vegetables start to sweat. Pour in the devilled tomato sauce and coat all the vegetables. Quickly add in the chicken and mix well.

4. Finally add in the tomatoes and cook for 5 minutes (depending how crisp/cooked you like tomato wedges). Serve with French fries and beer for the perfect Lankan snack with friends!

Sri Lankans love devilled anything! This hot, saucy bite is a classic; always served in sports clubs and bars. I've made this recipe a little spicier by the addition of Sriracha instead of the traditional ketchup. The chicken can be substituted with beef, sausages or fish. If you are using fish, make sure it is meaty and filleted. If it is beef, use a steak-quality cut like sirloin or rib eye.

spicy lankan style devilled eggs

Serves **4, makes 8 halves** | Prep **20 minutes** | Time **20 minutes**

INGREDIENTS

4 fresh eggs

6 tbsps mayonnaise

1 tsp English or yellow mustard

1 tsp of Kashmiri red chilli powder

½ tsp sea salt

1 clove garlic

1 green chilli, finely chopped

6 stalks of coriander, finely diced

At every birthday party, either a child's or an adult's, one must serve the humble yet always delicious 'eggboat'. So put on your party hat and give these a whirl. These devilled eggs are a bit on the spicy side, but if you want them milder just use half a teaspoon of chilli powder. If you can, store the eggs in the fridge sideways the night before (so that the yolk comes into the centre of the egg, and the egg looks good when cooked).

METHOD

1. It is essential that the eggs are cold. Bring a large saucepan with water to a rolling boil. Carefully lower each egg, one at a time, into the water. Turn down the heat to maintain a gentle boil and cook for 10 minutes. Fill a medium-sized bowl with cold water and about 10–15 ice cubes. Remove the eggs and immerse them into the ice water bowl. Once cooled, peel the eggs.

2. Take a sharp knife and cut the eggs lengthwise directly in the middle. Remove the yolks into a small bowl without damaging the whites. Put the egg whites into the fridge to use later.

3. Using a fork, crumble the egg yolks and mix in the mayonnaise. Halfway through vigorously mixing in the mayonnaise, add the mustard. Once the mustard is well incorporated, add the red chilli powder.

4. In a pestle and mortar, pound the sea salt with the garlic clove to a fine paste, and add into the yolks and mix well. Add in the fresh green chilli and mix until the yolks acquire a smooth, mousse-like quality.

5. Remove the boiled egg whites from the fridge and fill the centres with a heaped 1½ tsps of the yolk mixture. Or use a piping bag and pipe the centres in. Finish all the eggs with a sprinkling of the finely chopped coriander stalks. Serve immediately. However, if you are preparing this for later, place the yolk mixture and the egg whites in the fridge till just before you need to serve.

Unawatuna Beach

Unawatuna beach was very much at the epicentre of my young adult life in Sri Lanka. There was not much to do in Sri Lanka growing up and so, my 'long weekends' would entail my friends and I driving 'down south' (aka the southwestern coast) to a beach town and spending the weekends swimming in refreshing turquoise waters, drinking beers and local rum whilst singing along to tunes and bathing in the island sun.

Unawatuna was charming even during the war; a beautiful cobalt-blue water bay, perfect for swimming. What made it even better was that there were barely any tourists unlike today. Strewn across the bay in the mid-noughties were beach bars and small food shacks painted in every colour of the rainbow. Aptly they had very tropical names like Happy Banana, Lucky Tuna, Kingfisher and Tataruga (whatever the last one means). At one end of the bay was a striking cliff adorned with a Buddhist temple, which made for perfect viewing from Lucky Tuna. Along any part of the bay, you were treated to a sunset painted in vibrant colours of pink, neon orange, shades of purple and light blue.

Food on the beach in Sri Lanka is notoriously basic, so it is odd that one of the recipes in this book would be inspired by a dish that was introduced to me by my friend Rajinda—a simple fried fish dish that he would get the Happy Banana bar staff to make. It was a very stripped-back plate, just fresh kingfish cut into cubes, deep fried and served with raw onions and lashings of lime juice. Beach snack perfection!

I've improved the dish and changed the recipe a smidge, but I think anyone would be happy with this yum 'beach bite', perfect to be shared over ice-cold beer with friends.

fish fry at the beach

Serves **2-4** | Time **20 minutes** | Ethnic Roots **Sinhalese**

INGREDIENTS

350g cod fillet or any white fish fillet, washed
4 shallots
120g cornflour
2 tsps turmeric powder
1 tsp coriander powder
1 tsp cinnamon powder
1 tsp chilli powder
1 tsp salt
5 tbsps of ghee
Juice of 1 lime

METHOD

1. Cut the cod fillet into 5cm cubes and set aside.

2. Chop the shallots into fine rounds, so that you have thin pieces of shallots to garnish the fish with.

3. Place the cornflour into a bowl and combine with turmeric, coriander, cinnamon powder, chilli powder and the salt.

4. Heat a frying pan, and then add 2 tbsps of the ghee and allow to melt. Dip the cubed cod into the seasoned cornflour, ensuring that it is well coated. Cook the fish in batches, ensuring that all sides are well browned. Each cube should cook within 4 minutes.

5. Once all the fish is cooked, place on a plate and garnish with the finely cut shallots and then finish off with lashings of fresh lime juice. Eat immediately.

hot butter cuttlefish

Serves **2-4** | Time **35 minutes** | Ethnic Roots **Chinese heritage**

INGREDIENTS

350g cuttlefish, cleaned

240ml vegetable or sunflower oil

1 egg white

2 tbsps sunflower oil

1 tsp white sugar

1 tbsp soy sauce

1½ tbsps Chinese chilli paste

50g butter

2 cloves garlic, minced

3 spring onions, halved, then cut into quarters diagonally

1 capsicum, sliced thinly on the diagonal

2 dried red chillies, chopped into 3 pieces

½ tsp salt

For battering, dry-whisk in a medium-sized bowl:

75g cornflour

75g potato starch or tapioca flour

2 tsps turmeric powder

1 tsp salt

This Sri Lankan favourite was introduced to me by my late close friend Jonathan Solomons, a Colombo legend. He was a half-Chinese, half-Sri-Lankan Burgher; in 1948, his Chinese grandparents set up the famous Chinese Dragon restaurant. I first tasted this excellent dish at his birthday party when I was 14; his mother had arranged an 'action station' where chefs were frying up mounds of fresh butter-battered spicy cuttlefish. Cleverly, his family also came up with a vegetarian option called 'HBM'—hot butter mushrooms. It is a memory I hold very dear to my heart; it was only apt that I was inspired to create my own version of these dishes.

METHOD

1. Prepare the cuttlefish by cutting it into 2 x 1-inch pieces and then score each piece in a crisscross pattern. Pat dry, make sure that they have no moisture.

2. Heat the oil in a medium-sized saucepan, making sure that the oil is under two-thirds full. When the oil reaches 190°C, it is ready.

3. Arrange two bowls, one with the egg white and one with the flour dredge next to each other. Dip the cuttlefish one piece at a time into the egg white, shake off the excess and then immediately dip into the flour mixture, making sure each piece is fully but evenly dredged in the seasoned flour.

4. Batch-fry the dredged cuttlefish for 2–3 minutes at a time or until the cuttlefish has turned a light golden colour. Once golden, immediately remove from the oil and drain excess oil on a paper towel. Continue until all the cuttlefish is fried.

5. In a small bowl, mix the sugar, soy sauce, 1 tablespoon of oil and 1½ tablespoons of Chinese chilli paste together until a sauce is formed. Set aside to use in the next step.

6. In a wok, heat 1 tablespoon of oil over a medium fire and quickly melt the butter (avoid burning the butter). Next add in the minced garlic, and fry for 1 minute. Next add in the soy sauce chilli paste mix and cook for 2–3 minutes.

7. Next, add in the fried cuttlefish, spring onions, sliced capsicum, ½ teaspoon salt and dried chillies. Cook for 3 minutes, tossing constantly, making sure all the ingredients are well incorporated. Take off the heat and serve immediately.

chicken curry puffs

Serves **20 puffs** | Time **1 hour 10 minutes** | Ethnic Roots **British heritage**

INGREDIENTS

500g store-bought puff pastry

25g butter

½ red onion, minced

100g carrots, cubed into small pieces

3 cloves of garlic, minced

350g minced chicken

1½ tbsps of unroasted curry powder

1 tsp turmeric powder/paste

1½ tsps salt

1 tsp ground black pepper

 2 tsps tomato paste

180ml heavy cream

300g potatoes, peeled, boiled and roughly mashed

All-purpose flour for dusting

1 egg, beaten, used as egg wash

30ml of milk for the egg wash

2 tsps sesame seeds for garnishing (optional)

This dish is inspired by a very popular Sri Lankan short eat, a chicken pie. These are cupcake-sized puff-pastry pies filled with chicken and potato, and sometimes some white sauce. I added a twist by using cream and curry powder (to keep it Lankan)! These entail a little bit of fussy work, but I make them in big batches and freeze them, so I can pull them out as a quick snack or little bites when friends visit.

METHOD

1. If your puff pastry is frozen, thaw till it reaches room temperature. Preheat the oven to 180°C.

2. In a non-stick frying pan, melt the butter over a medium heat and quickly add in the onions and sweat them for 1 minute before adding the carrots. Fry for 2–3 minutes until the onions and the carrots start to caramelize. Add in the garlic and fry for another minute, mix well before adding in all the chicken.

3. Brown the chicken for 3 minutes. Mix in the unroasted curry powder, turmeric, salt, pepper and tomato paste. Cook for 4–5 minutes, until the chicken is golden brown.

4. Add the heavy cream into the chicken filling and mix well. This should start to form a thick sauce. Cook for 2 minutes before adding in the roughly mashed potato. Mix all the ingredients well and cook for a further 3–4 minutes until you have a moist chicken filling (most of the cream should be evaporated but the filling should stick together).

5. Dust your rolling surface with AP flour and roll out your pastry until it is 1cm thick. Cut 10cm x 10cm squares (I usually use a wooden ruler and a very sharp knife for this). You should get about 20 squares by rolling any off-cuts back together and cutting squares from the leftovers.

6. To fill, lightly roll each cut square a little bit to make sure you have a good amount of pastry to encase your filling. The aim is to make cute triangle-shaped puffs. Put a dining tablespoon of filling (25g) diagonally in the middle of the pastry, forming a small, flat triangle in the centre facing one pointed end of the square. Brush the edges of the sheet with a little egg wash using a pastry brush. Then take one diagonal edge and press it against the other edge, forming a triangle; press the edges together, applying a small amount of pressure with your fingertips. Using a fork, crimp the edges of the triangle puff for decoration. Prep all your curry puffs. Add the milk to the egg wash and mix well. Brush all the tops of the puffs with it and garnish with sesame seeds. Bake for 15 minutes or until golden brown.

prawn patties

Makes **15** | Time **1 hour 25 minutes** | Ethnic Roots **Portuguese heritage**

INGREDIENTS

For the shortcrust pastry:

300g all-purpose flour

1 tsp baking powder

1 tsp fine salt

125g cold butter, cubed

100ml ice-cold water

Extra flour for dusting

For the filling:

250g of peeled raw prawns

1 tsp baking soda

1 tsp salt

200g potato, boiled and slightly mashed

50g coriander leaves and stems, finely chopped

2 tsps unroasted curry powder

2 garlic cloves (20g), grated

10g fresh ginger, grated

Juice of 1 small lime (2 tbsps)

½ tsp turmeric powder

500ml frying oil—vegetable or sunflower.

METHOD

1. In a bowl, dry-whisk the flour, baking powder and salt. Next, add in the cubed cold butter. Work quickly to rub the butter into the flour until you have a wet, coarse sand texture, incorporating all the butter into the flour. Try to keep your hands as cold as possible when you do this, so as to not melt the butter.

2. Next, add in the ice-cold water, little by little, and start to build the dough. Knead the dough for at least 5–8 minutes, making a smooth ball. Use your palm to stretch the dough as you need. Once you have a smooth dough ball, shape it into a round disc and cover in cling film. Place in the fridge to rest for at least one hour.

3. Marinate the prawns in a bowl with baking soda and 1 teaspoon of salt. Mix well and set aside for 10 minutes before cutting into small 1cm pieces.

4. In a bowl mix the mashed potato, the marinated prawns, the minced coriander leaves and stems, curry powder, garlic, ginger, lime juice and the turmeric powder. Mix well and set aside.

5. Dust the work surface with some flour. Place the disc on your floured surface and roll out the dough into a flat 3mm-height piece. Make sure you rotate the dough as you roll for an even surface. Using a 9cm biscuit cutter, start to cut dough circles. You should have around 15 wrappers or maybe a few more.

6. Fill a small bowl with cold water. Take a wrapper and flatten the edges a little more with your fingers. Then take 1 tbsp of prawn filling and place it in the centre of the wrapper. Dip one finger in the cold water and brush one half of the wrapper with the water. Using your thumb and index finger press the two edges together to close the patty. Use a fork to crimp the edges. Repeat for all the wrappers.

7. In a deep saucepan, heat the oil over a medium heat. Once the oil has come to temperature, add 3–4 patties at a time, being sure not to overcrowd the pan. Fry for 4–6 minutes until they are golden brown, and the pastry has a bubbly surface to it. By this time, the filling will also be cooked. Continue to batch-fry and drain on paper towels. You can freeze the uncooked patties by separating each layer of patties with parchment paper; simply defrost before frying. They can be stored for 3 months in the freezer.

cassava chips

Serves **2-4** | Prep **15 minutes** | Time **10 minutes**

INGREDIENTS

450g cassava, washed and peeled

1 litre vegetable oil or coconut oil

3 tsps salt

2 tbsps red chilli powder

Cassava chips (or manioc chips) is a Sri Lankan street food staple. We love eating this by the beach or famously at the Galle Face Green in Colombo. I have many wonderful memories as a young kid of being on the green, eating manioc chips from a local cart and flying kites—a typical Sunday affair in Colombo. A great snack and a much better alternative to your pack of crisps.

METHOD

1. Use a mandolin or a knife to thinly slice the cassava. The thinner the slice, the better the chip will be, and quicker the frying time. Dry the cassava slices with paper towels or a dish cloth to absorb any excess moisture.

2. In a deep saucepan or a deep fryer, heat the oil over a medium-high heat. Bring the temperature of the oil to 180ºC. Add the cassava in batches, ensuring not to overcrowd the pan. Fry for 3–4 minutes, ensuring that the chip is golden and crispy. Be careful not to burn it (where it turns dark golden-brown). If your slices are very thin (almost 2mm thick) than the chips will fry very quickly, so this step requires judgement. Drain the cooked crisps on paper towels.

3. Whilst the slices are hot, put them in a bowl and add the salt and chilli powder. Toss, ensuring all the chips are coated. Serve warm.

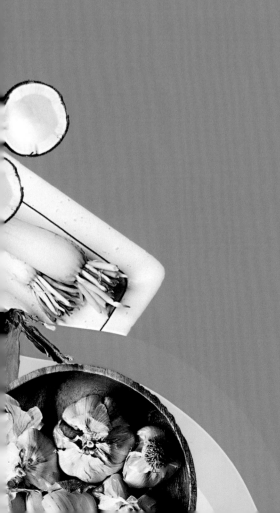

Soups and Kandas

To kanda or not to kanda? Or to simply soup?

Kandas are Sri Lanka's version of a nutritious porridge, one that can take many forms—from a kanji to a green rice soup. Every kanda has different health benefits. A kanji is often eaten with dates for Iftar during the month of Ramadan, as it is easy on the digestive system and full of slow-releasing nutrition. A kola kanda has different benefits depending on the leaf you use; curry leaves for managing high cholesterol or centella leaves for increased memory. Soups and broths are also important parts of the Lankan diet, from the famous Malay oxtail soup to the rasams and mulligawtany of the Tamils; every Lankan loves a soup. One of my childhood favourites, heavily advertised in the late 1980s and early 1990s, was marmite soup—a heaped tablespoon of umami-rich marmite diluted in a cup of hot water—instant satisfaction!

All the recipes in this section are great and, in my family, often exclusively eaten for breakfast. So if you like an aromatic spiced brekkie, give these a go!

my aunty-inspired chicken kanji

Serves **4-6** | Time **1 hour 20 minutes** | Ethnic Roots **Ceylon Moor**

INGREDIENTS

To prepare the chicken

600g chicken thighs, skin on

½ tsp turmeric powder

½ tsp salt

Have ready

2 tbsps sunflower oil/ coconut oil

100g red onion, roughly chopped

6 inches of pandan leaf, roughly torn

20 curry leaves

1 tbsp cumin seeds

1 tsp fenugreek seeds

2 tsps whole peppercorns

200g carrot, peeled and chopped into 10cm pieces

180g celery, chopped into 10cm pieces

1 tbsp garlic paste

½ tbsp ginger paste

1 chicken stock cube

1 litre of water

200g raw red rice or raw white rice, washed

400ml thin coconut milk

200ml thick coconut milk

2 tsps flaked sea salt

40g garlic, peeled and roughly chopped

3 cardamoms, pounded

My Aunty Mumtaz is one of the best cooks I have ever known—I dream of her food almost daily. When Ramadan comes around (or if anyone is ill) she whips out this delicious rice porridge, which is also really good for you. My recipe will never be as good as hers, but it is pretty close!

METHOD

1. Remove the chicken skins from the thighs and stretch onto a lined baking tray. Cover with another baking tray to flatten and cook in a 180°C oven for 30 minutes or until golden brown and crispy. Set aside for garnishing.

2. Massage the turmeric and salt into the washed chicken.

3. In a large pot or a pressure cooker, add the oil and bring to temperature over a medium heat. Add the onion, pandan, curry leaves, cumin seeds, fenugreek, peppercorns, cardamoms, carrots, celery and temper for 3–4 minutes until the spices are aromatic and the onions are starting to sweat. Next, add the garlic and ginger pastes and cook for 2 minutes before adding the chicken, and brown for 5 minutes.

4. Meanwhile, dissolve the chicken stock cube in the litre of water. Set aside.

5. Finally, add in the washed rice and garlic, stir-fry for 2–3 minutes, mixing well, and then add in chicken stock and the 400ml of thin coconut milk and cook covered for 30 minutes (stirring every 10 minutes) or 4 turns on the pressure cooker.

6. Next, add the thick coconut milk and the sea salt and mix well. Cook uncovered for 15 minutes until a thick porridge is formed.

7. Take out the chicken thighs, shred the chicken, remove the bones and mix back into the kanji. Serve in bowls and garnish with chicken skin crisps.

karapincha kola kanda (curry leaf porridge)

Serves **2-4** | Time **1 hour 20 minutes** | Ethnic Roots **Sinhalese**

INGREDIENTS

370g thick coconut milk

80g curry leaves, washed

140g red rice, washed a few times

40g garlic

30g fresh ginger, grated

1 tsp salt

800ml thin coconut milk (400ml canned coconut milk, 400ml water)

You can make this Sri Lankan breakfast staple with a variety of different leaves—centella, spinach; anything nutritious, really! This is a curry leaf-based recipe which is supposed to help control cholesterol! If you don't have a pressure cooker, step 2 can easily be done in a saucepan but it will take about 30–40 minutes to boil and soften the rice.

METHOD

1. Blend together the thick coconut milk and the curry leaves until the milk turns bright green in colour. Strain it through a sieve and squeeze out all the liquid from the pulp. Discard the residue and set aside the green coconut milk.

2. In a pressure cooker, put in the rice, garlic, grated ginger, salt and thin coconut milk. Stir and cover the pressure cooker with its lid. Put over medium to high heat and cook for 10–15 minutes (until 4 whistles have gone off). Allow the pressure to escape the cooker and open it carefully. Allow to cool for a few minutes.

3. Take half the rice porridge and half the green coconut milk and blend together for 1 minute, until the rice has been ground down. Add this back to the remaining rice porridge and mix well. Next, add the rest of the green coconut milk and mix. Put the pan back on a high heat and cook for 5 minutes, stirring continuously, till it starts to boil. Serve with a little piece of jaggery on the side if you need to cut through the taste.

chicken mulligatawny

Serves **2-4** | Time **1 hour 20 minutes** | Ethnic Roots **Indian Tamil**

INGREDIENTS

For the thickener

30g toor dhal soaked in 100ml water

30g rice soaked in 100ml water

2 tbsps cooked rice

For the curry paste

1 heaped tbsp whole black peppercorns

2 tbsps coriander seeds

4 whole dried red chillies

4 cloves

8 curry leaves

½ quill of cinnamon (2-3g)

30g garlic cloves, chopped

30g ginger, chopped

For the soup

2 tbsps coconut oil

2 bay leaves

1 red onion, finely chopped

1 tsp turmeric powder or paste

2 whole chicken legs, skinless, divided into thighs
and drumsticks

1½ tsp salt

1 litre chicken stock

100ml thick coconut milk

A handful of coriander leaves for garnishing

*Mulligatawny is a dish that is synonymous with
my childhood. Although very much consumed
as a soup, I used to love to pour thick lashings
of the soup over my stringhoppers and eat it
with heaps and heaps of pol sambol. Perfect
for battling a flu, this was my family's version
of a Jewish chicken soup, our own Sri Lankan
penicillin.*

METHOD

1. Soak the toor dhal and rice in water for at least 30
minutes, then drain. In a food processor, grind the
toor dhal, soaked rice and 2 tbsps of cooked rice into a
smooth paste.

2. Dry roast the black peppercorns, coriander
seeds, dried red chillies, cloves and curry leaves for
3 minutes, or until they start to brown and smell
aromatic. Set aside to cool.

3. Grind the roasted spices and curry leaves, cinnamon,
chopped garlic, chopped ginger to a smooth paste. Add
a little water if you find it is not grinding down, 2 tbsps
at a time. Set aside.

4. In a stockpot or a heavy-bottomed saucepan, heat 2
tbsps of oil over a medium heat. Add in the bay leaves,
onion and fry for 2 minutes or until the onions soften.
Add in the turmeric powder, chicken pieces and sauté
for 2 minutes before adding the curry paste. Cook for a
further 4-5 minutes until the meat starts to brown and
the curry paste starts to cook out.

5. Mix in the salt, the thickener and cook for a further
3-4 minutes. Next, add in the chicken stock and cook
covered for 15 minutes. Stir in the coconut milk and
cook for a further 5-10 minutes until a thick soup is
formed. Serve the chicken pieces whole or shredded
off the bone, garnished with some freshly chopped
coriander leaves.

rasam

Serves **2-4** | Time **25 minutes** | Ethnic Roots **Colombo Chetty/ Ceylon Tamil**

INGREDIENTS

For the rasam paste blend

30g shallots

10g garlic cloves

1 tsp cumin seeds

1 tsp coriander seeds

½ tsp peppercorns

½ tsp red chilli flakes

1 tbsp tamarind paste/ concentrate

¾ tsp salt

15 curry leaves

40ml water

¼ tsp turmeric paste/ powder

For the soup

740ml water

1 tsp coconut oil

¼ tsp mustard seeds

10 curry leaves

2 tbsps of coriander leaves and stems, chopped

METHOD

1. Grind all the ingredients to make a rasam paste until smooth.

2. Add the 740ml water to the rasam paste and mix well. Set aside.

3. In a deep saucepan over medium to high heat, heat the coconut oil and add the mustard seeds and the 10 curry leaves. Fry for 1 minute.

4. Next, add the rasam water into the saucepan and cook over a high heat for at least 5 minutes. Once it boils, add the coriander leaves and take off the heat. Stir quickly and serve immediately in bowls or teacups.

sago pudding

Serves **2** | Time **40 minutes** | Ethnic Roots **Ceylon Moor**

INGREDIENTS

1 litre water

250g small tapioca pearls

300ml coconut milk

100g jaggery, grated or very soft

2 cardamoms, pounded

2 pinches of salt (1/8 tsp)

Sago pudding is something that my family (the Marikkar side) makes so well. My aunts make it for me because they know it's my favourite, and it is also made for celebratory occasions like Ramadan and Hajj. It can be eaten on its own or spooned over a mountain of stringhoppers and eaten as a sweet treat! Give this a go and go heavy on the jaggery for a deep, rich taste.

METHOD

1. In a deep saucepan over a high heat, boil 1 litre of water. Once the water is boiling, lower the heat to medium and add the tapioca pearls, slowly stirring every few minutes for 15 minutes. The pearls should be translucent at the end of the cook and the water should turn thick and soupy.

2. Strain the pearls and wash them with running cold water. Set aside after draining.

3. In a bowl, mix the coconut milk and the jaggery until thoroughly combined, when the milk turns brown in colour.

4. In a deep saucepan, over a medium heat, add the sweetened coconut milk and heat for a minute. Next, tip in the strained tapioca pearls, cardamom pods, salt and mix well. Whisking continuously, cook for 5–8 minutes for the sago mixture to thicken. It is ready when it reaches a porridge-like thickness. Cool for 5 minutes before serving or eat cold after keeping in the fridge for at least 3–4 hours.

Rice and Gravy-Pullers

Lankans, if they were given the choice, would eat a mountain of rice for breakfast, lunch and dinner; according to the Food and Agriculture Organization, Lankans consume a massive 107kg of rice per capita. There are so many celebrations in Sri Lanka where special rice preparations are a critical part of the ceremonies; like biryani for Ramadan and weddings, yellow rice for Christmas and Sunday lunch, kiribath for auspicious events and the seven rice dishes for Valaikaapu to bless pregnant Tamil women before they give birth. As Robert Knox observed at the end of the 17th century, 'The main substance with which they fill their bellies is rice, the other things are but to give it a relish.'

One of the most wonderful aspects of Sri Lankan food is that most of the breads and rice dishes are gluten-free. However, this said, one cannot ignore the huge variety of rotis made from whole wheat and processed flour, much less our obsession with instant noodles. From godamba roti, pol roti, to parathas, there so many breads in the Lankan diet. One of the most notable is kade paan, the local bread loaf made in firewood-oven bakeries across every city, town and village; a staple for many households. Kade paan is often eaten as a breakfast or dinner meal with pol sambol and aromatic dhal, which is a perfect vehicle to mop up perfect mouthfuls of both.

As rice and breads are critical to meals in our cuisine, it dictates the curries and sambols that are served. There is no meal without the gravy-puller being at the centre of it. And although this section is just a taster, I hope it will be a good introduction to how Lankans eat.

kaha baath (yellow rice)

Serves **4-6** | Time **40 minutes** | Ethnic Roots **Sinhalese**

INGREDIENTS

400g short-grain rice (keeri samba or white raw rice)

1½ tsps turmeric powder

480ml coconut milk

5 cardamoms, pounded

10 cloves

6 inches of pandan leaf, torn

6 curry leaves

480ml water

1 cinnamon stick, broken into three large pieces

Arguably Sri Lanka's most famous rice preparation—yellow rice is a staple celebratory rice dish often served for big family occasions (like a Sunday lunch)! Long-grain rice can also be used, but short is best!

METHOD

1. Wash your rice three times, ensuring that the water runs clear. Drain and set aside.

2. Put all the ingredients in a deep saucepan or a rice cooker. If using a rice cooker, follow the normal cooking settings. In the pan, bring the rice and water to a boil.

3. Once the water is boiling, immediately turn it down to the lowest heat and allow it to simmer, covered with a lid until all the coconut milk and water has evaporated, approximately between 15–20 minutes.

4. Take off the heat and allow the rice to steam, covered, for another 10–15 minutes. Check that the grains are fully cooked. Serve with a black chicken or pork curry and pol sambol!

lankan chinese fried rice

Serves **4-6** | Time **50 minutes** | Ethnic Roots **Chinese heritage**

INGREDIENTS

To marinate the chicken (at least 30 minutes):

100g diced chicken breast

½ tsp salt

½ tsp pepper

½ tsp sugar

1 tsp soya sauce

1 tsp fish sauce

Prepare

4 eggs, yolks and whites separated

500g long-grain rice or jasmine rice, cooked the previous day

4 tbsps sesame oil

1 shallot, finely diced

20g garlic paste

20g ginger paste

1 large carrot, finely diced

½ large leek, finely diced

3 spring onions, finely diced

1 tsp dried chilli flakes

Sri Lankans love Chinese food. During the late 1980s and 1990s, going out to eat would invariably mean ending up in a Chinese restaurant. And Sri Lankans especially love Chinese fried rice. They order it by the truckload and consume it with vats of Chinese chilli paste. Sri Lankans will eat fried rice with curry too! However, this is in no way authentic Chinese. I have developed a simple but yum Chinese fried rice recipe; feel free to adapt it by adding prawns and pancetta too; approximately about 100g of each in step 3, but make sure that you allow it to cook for a further 4 minutes before step 4 to ensure that your meat and seafood is well cooked through.

METHOD

1. In a medium bowl, add the egg yolks and day-old cooked rice. Carefully mix or fold them together ensuring that you do not break the rice grains.

2. Heat 1 tablespoon of sesame oil in a large wok over a medium flame. Sauté the diced chicken for 4–5 minutes till golden brown and cooked through. Set aside.

3. Add another 2 tbsps of sesame oil to the same wok and start to bring the oil to temperature. Add the shallot, cook for 2 minutes before adding in the garlic and ginger paste and the carrot.

4. Mix in the leeks, spring onions, cooked chicken, dried chilli flakes and sauté for 2–3 minutes.

5. In the wok, push the chicken and vegetables to one side, making sure half the pan is clear. Add 1 tbsp of sesame oil and heat. Once hot, you need to work fast, add the egg whites and cook it on the clear side. After 30 seconds, mix the egg ensuring that you are creating ribbons of scrambled egg to dot the rice through. Continue till the egg is just cooked through.

6. After the egg is softly cooked, immediately add in your yolk-coated day-old rice. Work fast, making sure that you are folding the rice, chicken, vegetables and egg together. Fry for another 3–4 minutes, constantly stirring. Turn off your hob, and serve hot. It's ready to eat with some Chinese chilli paste!

pol roti (coconut roti)

Serves **5 rotis** | Time **50 minutes** | Ethnic Roots **Sinhalese**

INGREDIENTS

140g all-purpose flour

75g freshly grated coconut

20g red onion, finely minced

2 small fresh green chillies, finely minced

8 curry leaves, finely minced

1 tsp sea salt

1 tbsp coconut oil

75ml of warm water

METHOD

1. In a bowl, add all the ingredients except the warm water. Mix well to ensure even distribution of the ingredients throughout the flour.

2. Add the warm water and using a wooden spoon, mix it well making a dough. If it feels a little dry add another tablespoon full of warm water.

3. Very carefully use your hands, knead the dough until it comes together, for about 5 minutes.

4. Next, divide the dough into 5 equal pieces and roll into balls (60–65g each). Using a lightly floured surface, take one ball at a time and flatten the roti into a circle using your hand. Each roti should be about 1cm thick.

5. Heat a non-stick frying pan over a medium fire and rub a paper towel with a little coconut oil on the pan. Once hot, start cooking one roti at time. Cook each side for 2–3 minutes or until there is a little dark charring. Repeat for every roti, ensuring you lightly oil the pan between each roti. Serve with lunu miris and fish curry!

tasha's 'fool-proof' chicken biryani

Serves **6-8** | Time **2 hours** | Ethnic Roots **Ceylon Moor/Indian Tamil**

INGREDIENTS

For the marinade, blend the following to a fine paste:

4 cloves

10 small garlic cloves

30g ginger, peeled and diced

3 dried red chillies, stems removed

3 tbsps roasted curry powder

1½ tbsp chilli powder

1½ tbsp turmeric powder

1 cinnamon quill (5-7 g)

1 red onion, roughly chopped

8 curry leaves

1 tsp mustard seeds

1 tsp fenugreek seeds

240g of Greek yoghurt /natural yoghurt/buffalo curd

1 tsp salt

Prepare

800g boneless chicken thighs/ substitute: diced boneless chicken breast

600g potatoes, washed, peeled and diced into 1-inch cubes/ even cubes

1 tsp salt

For the rice:

5 tbsps ghee or oil

2 shallots, finely diced

1 tsp cumin seeds

1 tsp mustard seeds

500g basmati rice, washed of excess starch

1100ml water

2 chicken stock cubes

METHOD

1. Marinate the chicken for at least 1 hour. You can make the chicken marinade up to 3 days ahead and store it in the fridge.

2. Heat a little ghee or oil in a deep pan. Add in the shallots, cumin seeds, mustard seeds and fry for 3 minutes or until the shallot turns tender. Mix in the rice. This should be a further 3-4 minutes.

3. At this stage you can either transfer the rice, into a rice cooker, or leave it in the pan. To the rice add 800ml of water. Dissolve the 2 stock cubes into 300ml of warm water and add into the rice. Add 2 tbsps of ghee, turn up the heat and bring to a boil. Once the rice is boiling, turn down the heat and watch the rice until all the water has evaporated. Fluff up the rice by forking it. Set aside.

4. Whilst the rice is cooking, in a separate frying pan, put three tablespoons of ghee and fry the potatoes until golden and cooked through. These may have to be cooked in batches depending on the size of the pan. Season with salt.

5. Finally, take an ovenproof dish and put a layer of the marinated raw chicken with extra marinade on the bottom of the dish. Add a layer of the fried potatoes over the chicken. Put a layer (1 to 1½ cm height) of the cooked rice over the chicken and potatoes. Repeat this process, ending with a final layer of rice. There should be 3 equal layers of rice. Cover the dish with foil and place in a preheated oven at 180°C and cook for 30 minutes.

6. Remove the dish from the oven and check that the chicken is cooked through. If required, cook for a further 10 minutes lightly covered with the foil to ensure that the biryani is not drying out. Serve dressed with some quartered boiled eggs, roasted cashew nuts, fried onions, fried raisins and coriander for a finishing touch.

godamba roti

Serves **5 rotis** | Prep **2 hours 20 minutes** | Time **10 minutes** | Ethnic Roots **Indian Tamil/Malay**

INGREDIENTS

200g all-purpose flour
50ml milk
10g white caster sugar
10g salt
30ml coconut oil
70ml lukewarm water
Extra oil for roti making

Getting a godamba roti from a roadside kade was my ultimate joy when I was little—soft, thin, the size of two dinner plates were the prerequisites for the perfect one. With this recipe you can make them at home; it is not the same quality as a kade's but it's a good beginner's recipe. A godamba master can make about 10 rotis a minute (maybe even more)! Give this a go even if you are a novice.

On the next page, I have a recipe for how to make your godamba roti into the much-loved chicken kotthu. This is another roadside kade classic. I loved eating this at 3 a.m. after a solid night of partying with friends, served with a side of fried chicken and an iced Milo. This was classic Lankan fare to ward off a hangover but also very much a comfort meal at the same time. A bit labour intensive, it can be substituted with cut-up pieces of paratha (but it's not the same). The kotthu is a dish that needs no accompaniments.

METHOD

1. Put the flour in a mixing bowl and make a well in the centre. Pour in the milk. Sprinkle the sugar and salt around the flour. Add 5ml of oil and 1/3rd of the water. Start to knead until you have a scraggly dough and then add slowly add in the water until the dough starts to form into a sticky ball. Next add 5ml of oil into your hand and start to knead well. After 3 minutes, add another 10ml into your hand and knead until you form a soft, smooth dough. Knead for a further 5–8 minutes.

2. Separate the dough into balls weighing approximately 65g each. Place them in a mixing bowl, coat with 10ml of oil and cover with a damp cloth. Let it rest for 2 hours.

3. Oil your work surface and your hands. The dough balls are very soft and can tear easily, so you have to work fast. Using your fingertips, press out a disc from the dough ball. Continue to work in a circle and gently apply pressure with your fingers to press out and form a roti a size of a dinner plate and about 2–3mm thick.

4. Heat a roti pan or a crepe pan. Grease the pan with some oil using a paper towel or simply use cooking spray. Carefully lift the godamba roti from one end and place on to the hot pan. Cook for 1–2 minutes on one side or until you see some golden bubbles/char on it and flip for another minute on the other side. Repeat for the rest of the dough balls.

Tip: If you own a freestanding mixer, follow the same method in step 1 using your dough hook attachment. You will still have to do step 2 and 3 by hand, but it is much less work for your arms!

chicken kotthu

Serves **4** | Time **2 hours** | Ethnic Roots **Ceylon Moor**

INGREDIENTS

3 tbsps sunflower oil

150g red onion, sliced thinly as half moons

3 garlic cloves, minced

150g carrot, cleaned and julienned

200g leeks, washed and julienned

2 eggs, lightly whisked together

400g godamba roti, cut into 6 x 1cm strips

1½ tbsps red chilli flakes

The shredded chicken curry as given below

1 tsp salt

METHOD

1. In a large wok or frying pan, heat 2 tbsps of oil over medium heat. Add in the red onion, garlic, carrots, leeks and sauté for 3 minutes. The temper will start to soften and lightly brown. Push the vegetable temper to the side, and on the free side of the pan, heat 1 tablespoon of oil. Once the oil is hot, pour in the beaten egg and cook for 30 seconds before scrambling it.

2. Add in the godamba roti strips and the red chilli flakes and mix well. Cook for a further 2 minutes, ensuring that the vegetables and egg are well tossed in with the roti strips.

3. Mix in all the shredded chicken, salt and 3/4th of all the gravy. Sauté for another 3–4 minutes until the roti strips and vegetables have absorbed the gravy from the chicken curry. The kotthu should be moist and soft.

4. Serve with a bowl of the extra gravy on the side.

kotthu chicken curry

INGREDIENTS

2 tbsps unroasted curry powder

2 tbsps chilli powder

6 pieces of chicken thighs on the bone
(approx. 500–600g)

1½ tsps turmeric powder

½ tsp salt

2 tbsps vegetable/sunflower/coconut oil

1 small red onion, diced

3 cloves of garlic, minced

1 inch fresh ginger (grated)

2 fresh green chillies, diced

½ stick cinnamon, broken into smaller pieces

10 curry leaves

200ml water

200ml coconut milk

METHOD

1. In a small frying pan, quickly dry-roast 1 tbsp of curry powder and 1 tbsp of chilli powder for 1 minute. Immediately add the roasted chilli and curry powders to the chicken with turmeric and salt. Set aside and marinate for at least 10 minutes.

2. Heat all the oil in a deep medium-sized pan over a medium fire. Once the oil is hot, fry the onion for 3 minutes before adding the garlic, ginger, fresh green chillies, cinnamon and curry leaves into the pan. Cook for 4 minutes.

3. Next, add the remaining curry powder, chilli powder and turmeric powder. The temper will start to look quite dry, so add a little water to this mixture.

4. After a couple of minutes, add the chicken thighs and brown. If you ever feel like the chicken is about to burn, add a little water.

5. Once the thighs have browned, add the remaining water and the coconut milk. Allow the curry to cook over a low fire for 30–40 minutes. Once cooked, there should be a thick gravy and succulent pieces of chicken. Shred all the meat and remove the bones. Set the gravy aside for making the kotthu.

pittu

Serves **2-4** | Time **40 minutes** | Ethnic Roots **Ceylon Tamil/Indian Tamil**

INGREDIENTS

250g white or red rice flour

1 tsp salt (5g)

100g freshly grated coconut

200ml water

METHOD

1. In a mixing bowl, combine the rice flour, salt and grated coconut. Mix the ingredients together by using your dominant hand in a claw position and running your hand through the flour in a circular motion quickly. Stop once all the coconut and flour are well incorporated.

2. The next step is a very slow process and requires patience. Pour a little water, about 1–2 tablespoons at a time, into your mixing hand and then using the same motion as above, mix in the water to the flour-coconut mixture. This should hydrate the flour and with the more water you add, small dough balls are formed. Repeat till you have finished the water.

3. Heat your pittu steamer for a few minutes until the water has started to boil. Carefully take the pittu bambu (or the elongated part of the steamer) and fill it with the pittu dough balls till 80 per cent of the bambu. Reattach to the steamer and steam for 3–5 minutes. Using the back of a wooden spoon, carefully push out the metal disc end of the pittu bambu, pushing the steamed pittu out as one long piece on to a serving dish. Repeat for the rest of the dough; this recipe should produce at least two long pittu pieces. Have a bowl or small jug of coconut milk ready to pour on the pittu to serve.

Lamprais

Burgher Aunties have been instrumental in keeping the food of their ancestors alive. One of the dishes beloved across the island is, of course, the incredible lamprais. Even though a Burgher dish, many other ethnicities have started to produce this commercially across the country. Most of the commercially produced lamprais available lack authenticity and can often be a 'baath packet' wrapped in a banana leaf—with only a chicken curry, the addition of fish cutlets and fried boiled eggs.

One of the most famous Burgher families, the Raymonds, are prominent undertakers in Colombo and well-famed for their family's authentic lamprais. I am lucky to know a close personal friend of the Raymonds, who gave me some of their 'Raymond stash' to try, so I could get a proper education in lamprais.

The Raymond lamprais was aromatic and packed with flavour. As per the traditional recipe, it had a layer of ham separating the base of the rice from the banana leaf and layered upon the stock boiled rice was a four-meat curry consisting of pork, chicken, beef and mutton. Unlike most lamprais in Lanka, this one had traditional Dutch-style frikkadels instead of fish cutlets and there was no boiled egg in sight. It had a brinjal and ash plantain curry as well as a small ball of prawn blachan tucked away on the side of the parcel.

I've spent a long time researching several famous lamprais recipes and developed one that does not require an army to make, and if you have the stamina, it allows you to make twelve to fourteen parcels in one day. This recipe is trying to be as traditional as possible, but some of the techniques and shortcuts I have created will ensure that anyone can give it a go.

To make a lamprais, there are nine components:

1. Prepared banana leaves
2. A slice of ham
3. Thick coconut milk
4. Dutch-style beef frikkadels
5. Four-stock rice
6. Prawn blachan
7. A chilli sambol
8. Fried ash plantain and brinjal
9. Four-meat curry

dutch-style beef frikkadels

Makes **32–36 meatballs** | Time **40 minutes** | Ethnic Roots **Burgher**

INGREDIENTS

150g stale white bread, crustless and torn into large pieces

200ml cold milk

1 tbsp ginger paste

1 tbsp garlic paste

3 eggs

1 tsp coriander powder

1 tsp cumin powder

1 tsp pepper

1 tsp nutmeg

2 tbsps sea salt

400g mince beef

2 tbsps of sunflower oil

METHOD

1. Thoroughly soak the bread in the milk. Pulse the soaked bread, ginger paste and garlic paste in a small food processor until everything is well incorporated.

2. Beat the three eggs together. Set aside.

3. In a large bowl, pour in the soaked bread mixture, add the rest of the ingredients except the minced beef and mix well.

4. Add the beef mince. Using your hands, lightly mix the meat into the ingredients ensuring that you do not overwork the meat, but ensure that the ingredients are well combined. The meat mixture might feel paste-like but it should be light and airy, yet firm enough to form a ball. If it is too runny, add more bread to give it more structure.

5. Wet your hands, and using your palms, start to roll and form 4cm (1.5 inch) meatballs. Set aside on a plate. Continue to roll until all the beef mince mixture is over.

6. In a non-stick frying pan, heat the oil over a medium fire. Start frying the meatballs in batches, making sure that they cook at least 1½ minutes on each side and are golden brown. Do not overcrowd the pan; continue to fry in batches until all are done. Set aside for assembling the lamprais. This can be done a day ahead and refrigerated until used.

four-stock rice

Makes **14 packs of lamprais** | Time **50 minutes** | Ethnic Roots **Burgher**

INGREDIENTS

2300ml water

2 beef stock cubes

2 pork stock cubes

2 chicken stock cubes

2 lamb stock cubes

150ml ghee, melted

12 cardamom pods, crushed

10 cloves

4 cinnamon quills

2 tbsps whole black peppercorns

1kg short grain rice (keeri samba)

This recipe is usually made by boiling the bones from all the meat that has been used in the lamprais meat curry and additional bones. Cleaning and cooking it this way is very labour intensive—so use stock cubes (it's a cheat but it makes the rice a cinch)! If you can't find pork or lamb stock cubes, just double up on the chicken and the beef. If you have any bones, or pork skin, simply put them into the rice whilst it is boiling as additional flavour boosters.

METHOD

1. Take 300ml of hot water and dissolve all the stock cubes. Add all the stock water and add it to the leftover two litres of room temperature water. Mix well so that all the stock cubes are fully dissolved. This will yield 2300ml stock.

2. In a large stock pot, heat the ghee over a low heat, and add the crushed cardamoms, cloves, cinnamon quill, peppercorns and simmer for 3 minutes.

3. Mix in the rice and fry for 3 minutes before adding the 2300ml of stock water. Cover the stock pot with a lid and turn up the heat. As soon as the rice comes to a boil, immediately turn down the heat to low and allow it to simmer until all the stock is evaporated. Once the stock is evaporated, take off the heat and then let it sit covered for 10 minutes before fluffing the rice with a fork. Allow it to cool. Remove the cardamom pods, cloves and cinnamon pieces before assembling the lamprais.

four-meat curry

Makes **curry for 14 packs of lamprais** | Time **2 hours 30 minutes** | Ethnic Roots **Burgher**

INGREDIENTS

For the lamprais spice mix, grind to a powder:

8 cardamoms

10 cloves

6 dry red chillies

3 tbsps coriander seeds

2 cinnamon quills (10g)

2 tbsps fennel seeds

2 tbsps cumin seeds

2 tsps whole black peppercorns

2 tsps fenugreek seeds

For the curry:

400g boneless beef rib meat or shin, cut into 2cm cubes

400g boneless lamb shoulder, cut into 2cm cubes

400g boneless chicken thighs, cut into 4cm cubes

400g pork belly, cut into 2cm cubes

3 tbsps of ghee

20 curry leaves

200g red onion, finely minced

1½ tbsps garlic paste

1 tbsp ginger paste

2 stalks lemongrass, bashed and cut into 2 pieces

2 tbsps red chilli powder

1 tbsp turmeric powder

400ml thick coconut milk

720ml water

2 tsps tamarind paste or concentrate

2 tsps salt

METHOD

1. Roast all the spices for the lamprais curry powder for 3–4 minutes on a non-stick frying pan over a medium-high fire till they turn a light brown. Take off the heat and set aside to cool. Grind all the roasted spices to a fine powder. This will be the base of your curry.

2. In a bowl, mix the beef, lamb, chicken and pork pieces together with half the ground spice mix. Marinate for 15 minutes.

3. In a deep stock pot, over a medium heat, melt the ghee. After 1 minute, add in the curry leaves and fry for 30 seconds. Add in the minced onion and fry for another 2 minutes. Add in the garlic paste, ginger paste, lemongrass pieces and temper for 3 minutes.

4. Next, add in the leftover spice mix, chilli powder and turmeric powder, mix and cook for another 2–3 minutes until well incorporated. If it is looking like it is starting to burn, add a little water (4 tablespoons).

5. Add in all the marinated meat and mix well. Cook for 4–5 minutes, then add in all the coconut milk and mix well, stirring and cooking for another 8 minutes.

6. Add the water and cook covered for another 10 minutes. Add in the tamarind paste and mix well. Add in the salt.

7. Turn the fire to a medium-low and cook covered for 1 hour. After an hour, remove the lid and cook uncovered for another 30 minutes until you are left with a thick, rich and aromatic meat curry. This should make 14 lamprais. Set aside until assembly. This can be made a day ahead of assembly.

chilli sambol

be warned, this is a very spicy sambol

Serves **14 lamprais packs** | Time **50 minutes** | Ethnic Roots **Burgher**

INGREDIENTS

480ml coconut milk

1kg red onion, cut into half moons

5 lemongrass sticks, pounded with the back of a knife, cut into big pieces

5 cinnamon quills, broken into 2 big pieces each

180g tamarind paste

4 tbsps red chilli flakes

4 tsps chilli powder

3 tbsps ground maldive fish (optional)

30g ginger paste

30g garlic paste

3 tsps salt

4 tsps coconut oil

50g brown sugar

METHOD

1. In a bowl, mix all the ingredients except sugar. Make sure to keep the cinnamon pieces whole for ease of removal. Ensure that onions are well coated in the tamarind and coconut milk.

2. Over medium heat, heat the coconut oil in a frying pan. Add in the marinated onion mixture and allow it to sweat. After 4 minutes, sprinkle in the sugar. Turn down the heat to a low. Caramelize the onions and cook for 10–12 minutes until the mix acquires a jam-like consistency.

3. The onions will take on a deep red colour, and once the coconut milk has evaporated, the chilli sambol is cooked. Remove the lemongrass and the cinnamon sticks. Set aside until assembly. This sambol can be prepared 2 days ahead of assembly.

prawn blachan

Serves **14 lamprais** | Time **20 minutes** | Ethnic Roots **Burgher**

INGREDIENTS

150g dried shrimp (kooniso)

250g freshly grated coconut

5 garlic cloves

30g ginger

4 shallots

1½ tbsps of red chilli powder

1½ tsps of salt

Juice of 1 large lime

Although the recipe is called prawn blachan, Sri Lankans use baby dried shrimp in it

METHOD

1. Wash and dry your dried shrimp well. It would be advisable to wash them at least three times as there tends to be excess sand and grit in them.

2. In a food processor, add all the ingredients and grind until you have a fine, bright orange paste. With wet hands, check the blachan to see if you can roll it into a 4cm ball. If you are able to, this means it is ready. If it is too dry, add a couple of tablespoons of water; if it is too wet, add some more dried shrimp. Set aside for lamprais assembly. This can be made up to 3 days ahead and stored in the fridge.

fried ash plantain and brinjal (kaliya) curry

Serves **14 lamprais** | Time **1 hour 20 minutes** | Ethnic Roots **Burgher**

INGREDIENTS

300g ash plantain, cut into 2.5cm (1-inch) cubes

700g eggplant/brinjal, cut into 2.5cm (1-inch) cubes

3 tsps salt

1 tsp turmeric paste or powder

240ml coconut oil for frying

200g whole small shallots, skins peeled, left whole

70g garlic, peeled and cloves left whole

10 fresh green chillies, stalks removed, left whole and halved

20 curry leaves

6 cardamoms

8 cloves

2 tsps mustard seeds

4 tbsps white vinegar or apple cider vinegar

2 tbsps white sugar

1 tsp table or sea salt

120ml thick coconut milk

2 tsps coconut oil for final fry

4 tsps red chilli powder

METHOD

1. In one bowl, mix 2 teaspoons of salt and ½ teaspoon of turmeric powder and massage into the brinjal. In another bowl, mix 1 teaspoon of salt and ½ teaspoon of turmeric powder into the ash plantain.

2. In a saucepan or a small wok, heat coconut oil over a medium–high heat. Test the oil with a skewer to see if it is hot (it will start to bubble around the skewer). Start batch-frying the brinjal till they turn a deep golden brown; this will take approximately between 7–8 minutes for each batch. Repeat for the ash plantain, they should also be very golden in colour. Set aside to drain on a paper towel.

3. In the same frying oil, add the shallots and fry for 3 minutes. Remove and drain on paper towel. Fry the garlic in the hot oil for 2–3 minutes until they turn just golden; remove and drain on a paper towel. Fry the green chillies for 30 seconds in the hot oil—the skins should blister. Remove and drain. Fry the curry leaves for 30 seconds and remove.

4. In a grinder, blitz the cardamom (whole pods), cloves and mustard seeds together until you have a fine powder. In a bowl, mix the vinegar, sugar and the spice mix together. Tip in the thick coconut milk and stir well to incorporate all the ingredients together.

5. In a fresh frying pan, heat the 2 teaspoons of coconut oil over a medium heat. Add the fried ingredients into the pan and fry for 2 minutes. Add in the red chilli powder and 1 teaspoon of sea salt. Cook for 2 minutes, and add in the thick coconut vinegar liquid. Be careful to fold the liquid into the fried ingredients as you don't want to smash the vegetables together. Continue to cook for 4 minutes until a thick jam-like curry is left. Set aside to cool for lamprais assembly.

How to assemble your lamprais

It is essential that all the elements are cooked and ready to go. You may need some kitchen string for fastening the lamprais packs.

THE BANANA LEAF

You need to have 8 rather large banana leaves; each side on either side of the leaf vein should have at least 30 cm width. Cut 25 x 35cm rectangles from the banana leaf. Wash the rectangles carefully and then dry them with a tea towel. Over a gas burner, turn on the largest burner to high and heat each leaf over the flame, for only few seconds. This makes the leaf more pliable, so it will not split when we fold the rice into the leaf.

ASSEMBLING THE LAMPRAIS

In the centre of the leaf, place one layer of thick ham (½–1cm thick) in the middle of the leaf. Take one packed cup of four-stock rice, place it on the top of the ham and in the middle of the leaf. Around the rice arrange 2 frikkadels, 2 serving spoons of the four-meat curry, 1 serving spoon of chilli sambol, 1 serving spoon of the kaliya curry and a 4cm ball of the prawn blachan, making sure that all the curries are separate from each other. Pour 2 tablespoons of thick coconut milk on top, in the middle of the rice. Bring both of the long lengths of the banana leaf together and make a thick middle fold. Next take the two ends of the lamprais and fold the ends like a birthday present. Fasten the assembled lamprais with string. If you are a little worried, you can wrap it in aluminium foil but this means that if you freeze your excess lamprais you may have to reheat them in the oven instead of steaming it.

BEFORE SERVING

Heat each lamprais by steaming them for 20–25 minutes in a steamer over boiling water. This is the best method. If you prefer, you can heat it in an oven at 180°C for 20 minutes. If you have frozen the lamprais, thaw it and follow the above instructions. If you are heating from frozen, minus an oven, then steam for a minimum of 40 minutes before serving.

hoppers

Serves **20-25** | Prep **12 hours** | Time **2 hours** | Ethnic Roots **Indian Tamil**

INGREDIENTS

420g white raw rice (sudu kekulu)

1200ml tap water (room temperature)

150ml coconut water (first water from the mature coconut)

25ml water

280ml thick coconut milk

¼ tsp baking soda

1 tbsp sugar

½ tsp salt

Arguably Sri Lanka's most coveted dish, there are no shortcuts or cheats with this recipe. It demands patience but the pay-off is fantastic: crispy, flavourful and authentic, what more could you ask for? Fermentation is key to getting this recipe right: do not allow your blended rice batter to ferment for over twelve hours. Do not attempt a shortcut by using rice flour, it won't result in a thin crispy hopper! This recipe makes quite a few hoppers, and considering the effort and time you put into making this, I think you should feast on them!

METHOD

1. Wash the white raw rice at least three times until the water runs clear. Strain and set aside. In a large bowl, place the washed rice and the 1200ml tap water, cover with a napkin and lid or plate. Allow to soak for 4 hours.

2. After four hours, strain the rice again and blend the rice with a 150ml of coconut water and 25ml water until you have a thick puree similar in consistency to a creamy soup. Place in a mixing bowl and cover again with a napkin and lid and allow it to ferment for a minimum of 6 hours, preferably 10-11 hours.

3. After the pureed rice has fermented, add in the coconut milk, baking soda, sugar and salt. Mix well with a soup ladle or a heavy-based spoon. Cover again with a napkin and lid and allow to ferment further for an hour.

4. Once the batter is ready, it is time to make the hoppers. Have a small plate with a neutral oil and a paper towel to lightly grease the inside of the hopper pan between cooks. Heat the hopper pan so that it is hot, add 3/4th batter of a soup ladle into the centre of the pan and try using your dominant hand to turn all the batter in one swirl around the edges of the pan, leaving a thin layer on all sides and a little extra batter in the centre. Cover with your hopper pan lid and cook for 2 to 3 minutes until you have a golden-brown crispy pancake with a fluffy doughy centre. Make sure to stir the batter between every cook of each individual hopper. Serve with lunu miris and fish curry.

Sunil Perera and the Gypsies

Most Lankans born before the early '90s remember witnessing our parents, extended family or parents' friends break out into heavily gestured dance moves when a baila song came on at a party or a wedding. Amazing moves like 'girl goes to the well' and 'girl carries water back from the well' and so forth. No one defines Lankan pop culture quite like Sunil Perera and the Gypsies. Always humorous, their music captured Sri Lankan culture—politics, love and most importantly food—unlike any other band in Sri Lanka. Sunil himself was a brilliant and outspoken man, always calling out politicians in his songs for their questionable behaviour. He was a Lankan treasure.

One of my favourite meals ever is stringhoppers. A stringhopper or 'indi appam' is a pressed rice noodle, which is steamed and usually served with pol sambol and kiri hodi. It is a meal that brings me unbridled joy and one that I request every time I am home. Add a Ceylon Moor meat curry with it and it is beyond delicious. Sunil and the Gypsies seem to share my sentiment, so much so that they wrote a cult classic about how much they love the meal themselves. So, when you try this meal, turn on YouTube and listen to the song whilst you gorge on indi appam!

Learn the words for yourself:

Piti kotapan

Piti kotapan none, Piti halapan none....
Pound the flour, my lady, sieve the flour, my lady

Heta udeta kannata mata indi aappan one
I want stringhoppers for breakfast tomorrow

Jam paan thawath kanna ba
I can't eat bread and jam any more

Kimbula banis kewath mata kisi gathiyak na
Eating Kimbula buns has no joy any more

Mun ata mata epa, kiri bath mata epa
I don't want mung beans , I don't want milk rice

Umbe athin rasata hadala
When you make it, it's so tasty

Indi appan tikak kanna
Just eat a few stringhoppers

Indi appa nikan kanna ba
You can't eat stringhoppers on its own

Kiri hodda nathuwa indi appe lissala yan na
'Kiri Hodi' is what helps the stringhoppers go down well

Umbala kada daala, samboleth hadala
Add some maldive fish, make a sambal

Mage doladuka niwalanna
To satisfy my cravings

Indi aappa tikak kanna
Just eat a few stringhoppers

Cookery pothe recipe wedak naha
No point of cookery book recipes

Oya ham bacon cheese butter mata dirawan na
I can't digest ham bacon cheese butter

Ane mokatada thawa katha
Please say no more

Ispeacial mukuth epa
No need for anything special

Mage aadare wedi wennai
My love just grows

Doladuka heta nethi wennai
So take away my cravings for tomorrow

stringhoppers

Makes **30–32 stringhoppers** | Prep **25 minutes** | Time **30 minutes** | Ethnic Roots **Indian Tamil**

INGREDIENTS

350g stringhopper rice flour

½ tsp salt

400ml room temperature water

A little neutral oil for greasing the stringhopper mats

Special equipment:

A stringhopper press

15 stringhopper mats

A steamer

If you are making this for kids, I'd add food colouring to make it more fun and serve the stringhoppers with sugar and lots of cold milk so that they can eat it as a style of cereal.

METHOD

1. In a large bowl, mix the stringhopper flour and the salt together, ensuring that they are well combined.

2. Slowly, add water about 50ml at a time until you get a wet dough that holds together but is soft to the touch.

3. Oil all the mats so that the noodles don't stick on them. Heat the steamer set over a high heat so that the water is boiling. Fill the stringhopper press with the dough and press over the mat in two circles covering the mat. Continue for 3–4 mats. Depending on the size of your steamer and saucepan, layer 4–5 noodled mats and steam for 4–5 minutes. Remove from the steamer and carefully pull the stringhopper noodle from the mat. Continue for the rest of the dough until you have made 30–32 stringhoppers.

kiribath (milk rice)

Serves **4** | Time **2 hours** | Ethnic Roots **Sinhalese**

INGREDIENTS

350g white raw rice (washed)

500ml water

1 tsp salt

390ml thick coconut water

Kiribath is an institution in Sri Lanka, often served to mark important occasions, like the Sinhala and Tamil New Year, the first day of every month for blessings and special life moments like moving into a new home or to celebrate an anniversary. Milk rice can be traced back to the royal courts of the Kingdom of Polannaruwa (1070–1215 AD); known by many names—Paayasa, Keerantha, Kiirodana. Most Lankans love their Kiribath, and it is often eaten savoury with a spicy chicken or fish dish or sweet with pani pol. We always eat it for breakfast, so put in a little extra effort and start your day like an ancient Sri Lankan king.

METHOD

1. In a deep saucepan, place the rice, salt and water and cook over a high heat. Cook for 4–5 minutes until the rice comes to a rolling boil and then reduce to a low heat and cook covered for 15 minutes or until all the water has evaporated.

2. Using a wooden spoon stir the rice, making sure to mash some of it and ensure it sticks together. To the cooked rice, mix in the coconut milk and cook on a low heat for a further 10–12 minutes. Stir every 4–5 minutes to prevent the rice from sticking to the bottom of the pan and burning. During the last minute, turn up the heat to high and mix the rice well. Check the seasoning of the rice, add more salt if needed.

3. Take a large serving plate, rub some thick coconut milk on top of it and quickly pour the rice mixture on the plate. Use a palette knife coated in coconut milk and start to form an even layer of milk rice (about 1–1.5 inches in height). Smooth out the top and then use a knife and cut into equal size pieces (10cm x 10cm squares or diamond shapes). Allow to cool and set for up to 30 minutes before serving.

Sambols

Sri Lankan food without sambol, I would argue, is a meal without heart. The sambol is related to a Malaysian and Indonesian 'sambal' and every meal in a Lankan household has at least one sambol dish.

The idea behind eating a sambol is to eat the little bit of it with your meal; however, they are a big favourite of mine and I usually pile them on to my plate. Some sambols are fiery, some are healthy, almost all are super nutritious and primarily served raw. A lot of sambols in Sri Lanka have raw grated coconut bases. Another key ingredient is lime; the juice is an essential part of finishing most sambol dishes.

Most Sri Lankans use sambols as a method to eat nutritious superfood leaves raw and get the best out of them. I urge you to read up, find greens available near you and use them by finely slicing them and mixing with coconut and lime juice!

a quick carrot sambol

Serves **2-4** | Time **20 minutes** | Ethnic Roots **Sinhalese**

INGREDIENTS

200g carrots, peeled and grated

50g red onion, sliced as half moons

1 large fresh green chilli, minced

1 tomato, chopped lengthwise

1 tsp maldive fish, pounded (substitute: bonito flakes or remove)

100g freshly grated coconut (optional)

Juice of 1 lime

1 tsp salt

METHOD

1. Combine all the ingredients in a bowl, except the lime juice and salt.

2. Just before serving, add the lime juice and salt and mix well, ensuring that all the ingredients are combined. Serve immediately.

This sambol is delicious with or without coconut. A very healthy, fresh, raw carrot side dish, this pairs very well with a rice and curry.

carrot top sambol

Serves **2** | Time **15 minutes** | Ethnic Roots **Sinhalese**

INGREDIENTS

50g carrot top leaves or centella asiatica leaves, finely minced

50g grated coconut

50g shallots, finely diced

½ tsp salt

3 green chillies, finely minced

Juice of 1 lime

METHOD

1. Place all the ingredients in the bowl, except the lime juice.

2. Just before serving, add the lime juice and mix well. Serve immediately.

One of our most famous dishes is a gotu kola (centella asiatica or brahmi) sambol—famed to improve one's memory, this is one punchy raw salad. However, since centella asiatica is not easily found globally, I substituted the leaves with carrot top leaves, which are super nutritious and something most people would throw away.

easy green pol sambol

Serves **2-4** | Time **25 minutes** | Ethnic Roots **Sinhalese**

INGREDIENTS

100g desiccated coconut

240ml tinned coconut milk

15g (4 large chillies) fresh green bird's eye chilli, sliced in half lengthwise

240ml boiling water

10g garlic, largely diced (3 cloves)

10g shallots, largely diced (2 shallots)

6–8 curry leaves, remove the stalks

½ tsp turmeric powder

1 tbsp water

Juice of 1 lime

1 tsp sea salt

Sri Lanka's most common pol sambol is orange in colour. This is another less common but extremely delicious version. The original recipe calls for pickled habanero chillies (nai miris); however, this recipe uses fresh green chillies and curry leaves. Furthermore, since it is really time-consuming to grate fresh coconut, this recipe uses desiccated coconut.

METHOD

1. In a bowl, mix the desiccated coconut with the coconut milk and set aside for 10 minutes. After absorbing all the coconut milk, the texture of the desiccated coconut will change and be wet to the touch.

2. Steep the fresh green chillies in the boiling water for 5 minutes. This will take the sting out of them. Drain and set aside.

3. In a food processor, add the garlic, shallots, green chilli, curry leaves, turmeric, a tablespoon of water and soaked desiccated coconut. Blend until the coconut starts to change colour and turns bright green. Once all the ingredients are half-blended, add in the lime juice, sea salt, and blend till all the ingredients are combined, but have not formed a paste. There should be green-stained coconut flakes. Serve with stringhoppers or white rice and crab curry.

pol sambol

Serves **2** | Time **15 minutes** | Ethnic Roots **Malay**

INGREDIENTS

2 tsps ground maldive fish (optional)

1 clove garlic

2 small shallots, roughly chopped

½ tsp salt

2 tbsps red chilli flakes

1 whole coconut, freshly grated (200-250g)

Juice of ½ large lime

Arguably, Sri Lanka's most famous sambol, pol sambol, is the most versatile—eat it with stringhoppers, hoppers, roti and rice, put it in a grilled cheese sandwich or eat it as part of a fry-up—it's a winner! When Tinie Tempah played my music festival in Colombo, we took his team and him to eat crab curry and pol sambol. His team described it as 'pure gold'. We even had to pack some frozen pol sambol for them to take back to the UK. If that's not a stamp of excellence, I don't know what is.

METHOD

1. Powder the maldive fish in a spice grinder and set aside.

2. In a pestle and mortar, pound the garlic, shallots and salt until you start to form the beginnings of a paste. Add in the chilli flakes, the grated coconut and the pounded maldive fish. Make sure you mix well and the grated coconut is turning orange.

3. Once all the ingredients are well-combined, pour in the lime juice and pound into the pol sambol and mix again. Serve with stringhoppers or yellow rice!

lunu miris

Serves **2-4** | Time **15 minutes** | Ethnic Roots **Malay**

INGREDIENTS

5 small shallots or 1 red onion, roughly chopped
1 clove garlic
½ tsp salt
2 tsps red chilli flakes
Juice of 1 lime

METHOD

1. In a pestle and mortar, pound the shallots, garlic and salt until you start to form the beginnings of a paste.

2. Add in the chilli flakes, lime juice and pound the ingredients together making sure you mix well.

I love lunu miris so much. I blame this particular sambol for my chilli addiction. Simply add 2 teaspoons of maldive fish to this recipe and voila, you have a katta sambol too.

mint sambol

Serves **2-4** | Time **20 minutes** | Ethnic Roots **Ceylon Moor/Indian Tamil**

INGREDIENTS

100 grams desiccated coconut
120ml thick coconut milk
60 grams mint leaves (no stalks)
30 grams coriander leaves and stems
2 fresh green chillies
Juice 1 lime
1 tsp of salt

Thinking of eating some biryani but you don't have the standard mint sambol? Fret not, here's my cheat recipe. No miris gala required but you will need a food processor or blender.

METHOD

1. In a bowl, mix the desiccated coconut in the coconut milk and allow it to soak for 5-10 minutes. Set it aside.

2. In a blender, put in all the remaining ingredients, along with the soaked desiccated coconut.

3. Blend till you make a fine semi-runny mixture. If you find the mixture is too thick, add more coconut milk. Finish by blending in the salt.

malay pickle

Serves **2-4** | Time **6 hours** | Ethnic Roots **Malay**

INGREDIENTS

1 carrot (130g), cut into 1 x 3cm batons

100g green capsicum (malum miris), cut into
1 x 3cm batons

2 fresh green chillies, chopped into large pieces

200g small shallots, cut into halves

250g dates, pitted

300ml hot water

2 garlic cloves, cleaned, peeled and chopped

120ml apple cider vinegar or white vinegar

1 tbsp mustard seeds

1 tbsp chilli powder

1 tbsp sugar

1½ tsps salt

2 tsps ginger paste

1 tsp black pepper

One of Sri Lanka's top pickles, no biryani is complete without this. A gift from the Malay community, this pickle has it all ... depth of flavour, sweet, sour and crunchy. Perfect with a kaha baath or even a regular rice and curry. Make this and store the excess in your fridge for a few weeks.

METHOD

1. Dry the vegetables with a towel before cutting them, else the pickle will not ferment correctly.

2. Soak the dates in the hot water, for 10 minutes. Next, peel the skins (as much as possible) off the dates. Cut each date into halves lengthwise or into quarters if your dates are already pitted.

3. Using a food processor or spice grinder, blend the garlic, 3 soaked dates (chopped), the vinegar, mustard seeds, chilli powder, sugar, salt, ginger paste and black pepper into a thick paste.

4. In a large bowl, put the carrots, green capsicum, the remaining cut dates, fresh chillies and the shallots. Add the blended paste and using a spoon mix all the ingredients well, ensuring that all the vegetables and date pieces are coated in the paste. Cover with clingfilm and a non-transparent lid and set aside to pickle for 2–6 hours before eating.

coconut mellum

Serves **2-4** | Time **20 minutes** | Ethnic Roots **Sinhalese**

INGREDIENTS

Grind together in a food processor:

200g freshly grated coconut

1 tsp turmeric powder or paste

1 garlic clove, largely diced

2 shallots, largely diced

1 tsp pepper

1 tsp salt

10 curry leaves

2 green chillies, largely diced

1 tsp maldive fish

1 tbsp water

For the temper:

1 tbsp coconut oil

1 tsp mustard seeds

½ cinnamon quill (5g)

1 piece pandan leaf, torn into small pieces

5 curry leaves

Unlike its pol sambol counterparts, this bright yellow coconut sambol is cooked. Delicious when paired with a Ceylon Moor beef curry and ghee rice!

METHOD

1. Pulse all the 10 ingredients together until you have a crumbly yellow coconut mixture.

2. Heat a frying pan over a medium fire, and bring the coconut oil to temperature. Add in the mustard seeds, cinnamon quill, pandan and curry leaves. Fry for 1–2 minutes before adding the ground yellow coconut mixture.

3. Fry the coconut mixture until it starts to dry out—approximately another 4–5 minutes. Serve as an accompaniment to pittu, stringhoppers or rice.

seeni sambol

Serves **2-4** | Prep **25 minutes** | Time **25 minutes** | Ethnic Roots **Sinhalese**

INGREDIENTS

120ml coconut milk
250g red onion, cut into half moons
1 lemongrass stick, pounded with the back of a knife, cut into big pieces
1 cinnamon quill
20 curry leaves
3 tbsps tamarind paste
2 tsps red chilli flakes
1 tsp chilli powder
2 tsps ground maldive fish (optional)
1 tsp salt
3 tsps brown sugar
1 tbsp coconut oil

METHOD

1. In a bowl, mix all the ingredients except the sugar and coconut oil. Ensure that onions are well coated in the tamarind and coconut milk.

2. Over a medium fire, heat a frying pan and add the coconut oil. Add in the marinated onion mixture and start to cook down the onions. After 2 minutes, sprinkle over the sugar. Cook for 8–10 minutes until the mix starts to acquire a jam-like consistency.

3. Once the onions turn brown and jammy and the coconut milk has evaporated, the seeni sambol is ready.

After pol sambol, it could be argued that a seeni sambol is one of Sri Lanka's most beloved side dishes. 'Seeni' simply translates into sugar and this sweet, caramelesque onion sambol is an essential accompaniment to many dishes—hoppers, kiribath and even pol roti.

pani pol

Serves **2-4** | Prep **25 minutes** | Time **20 minutes** | Ethnic Roots **Malay**

INGREDIENTS

175ml jaggery treacle
2 tsp dark brown sugar
3 cardamom pods, pounded
3 cloves, pounded
¼ tsp salt
¼ tsp whole black peppercorns, slightly pounded
300g freshly grated coconut

Pani pol is simply a sweet coconut sambol. This can be eaten in a multitude of ways—steamed inside a stringhopper to make lavaria, eaten with kiribath for a sweet meal instead of a spicy one, and wrapped inside a crepe to make a Lankan fav, pani pol pancakes.

METHOD

1. In a small saucepan, over a low to medium flame, add the jaggery treacle, the dark brown sugar and melt. After two minutes, add in the cardamom pods, cloves, salt and peppercorns. Cook for a further 3–4 minutes.

2. When the sugar is all dissolved, turn the flame down to low and mix the freshly grated coconut into the syrup. The coconut should absorb all the syrup and turn a dark brown colour. Continue to cook over a very low heat for another 4–5 minutes. The coconut should darken in colour and have a very soft and sticky texture. Serve with kiribath or pancakes!

bittergourd sambol

Serves **2-4** | Time **25 minutes** | Ethnic Roots **Sinhalese**

INGREDIENTS

250ml vegetable oil for frying

¼ tsp turmeric powder

1 tsp salt

250g bittergourd, washed and cut into 3mm rounds

4 shallots (20g), cut into 3mm rounds

3 large green chillies, cut into rounds

Juice of 1 lime

Bittergourd (aka bitter melon) is a sort of miracle vegetable that is a staple in the Sri Lankan diet. I personally love the taste, and it makes an excellent mild yellow curry too. The texture is not for everyone, but it is a superfood that has a whole list of health benefits. Packed full of Vitamin A and C, it is good for bone formation, wound healing, disease prevention, glowing skin and great vision.

Most Lankans, however, know that it is amazing for bringing down blood sugar. They make it into a health water, cutting slices of it and soaking it in water overnight so that it may be consumed in the morning before breakfast. My father, who vehemently denies having any kind of sugar problems (as he says he's borderline diabetic), was forced to undergo this natural treatment by my mother. It was a running joke that this water tasted less than ideal and was aptly nicknamed 'Snozzcumber' juice (a little BFG joke).

So, if you are having sugar problems, give this a go as part of your morning routine. I would also highly recommend getting your teeth into this sambol, it's unbelievably delish.

METHOD

1. Heat the oil in a small wok or hopper pan, over a medium high flame. In a small bowl, mix the turmeric powder and ¼ teaspoon of salt in with the bittergourd, ensuring that they are well-coated. Once the oil has come to temperature, start frying the bittergourd in batches for 3–4 minutes each, until they are brown and tender. Drain on a paper towel.

2. In a large bowl, mix the shallots, green chillies and the fried bittergourd slices together. Just before serving, add in the lime juice and the rest of the salt, and mix well. Serve with rice and curry.

banana blossom fry

Serves **2-4** | Time **40 minutes** | Ethnic Roots **Sinhalese**

INGREDIENTS

To prepare the banana flower:

700g banana flower

500ml water

1 tsp turmeric powder or paste

1 tsp salt

250ml vegetable oil for frying

For the temper:

3 tbsps coconut oil

1 red onion, thinly sliced as half moons

12 curry leaves

½ cinnamon quill (5g)

3 tsp ground/pounded maldive fish

½ pandan leaf, torn into pieces

3 tsp red chilli flakes

1½ tbsps tamarind paste

1 tbsp thick coconut milk

1½ tbsps sugar

½ tsp salt

METHOD

1. Remove the first three outer leaves and the stalk of the banana flower. Cut the flower in half and you will notice stamen inside the flower; all parts of the flower can be eaten, so mince into 1cm pieces. Place the minced flower pieces in a large bowl with the water, turmeric and salt. Using your hands, rub the banana pieces for at least two minutes to disinfect and clean the vegetable. Drain the banana flower and discard the water. Pat dry with paper towels to remove any excess moisture.

2. Heat the vegetable oil in a deep saucepan over a medium high flame. Add 1–2 large serving spoons of the banana flower and fry for 4 minutes until they start to look golden brown and crispy. Continue in batches. Drain the fried banana flower on a kitchen towel and set aside.

3. Over a medium high flame, in a large frying pan, heat the coconut oil for the temper. Add in the onions and fry for 3–4 minutes until they start to brown and get slightly crispy. Next, add in the curry leaves, cinnamon quill, the ground maldive fish pieces, the pandan leaves and cook for another 2 minutes.

4. Add in the fried banana flower pieces and fry further for a minute before adding the chilli flakes. Mix well for 2–3 minutes before adding in the tamarind paste, coconut milk and sugar. Cook down for another 3–4 minutes.

5. Season with ½ teaspoon salt, check and add more if needed. Fry for another couple of minutes until you have a crunchy sambol similar in texture to homemade Chinese chilli paste. Delicious when served with biryani, rice or stringhoppers!

raw mango achcharu

Serves **2-4** | Time **25 minutes** | Ethnic Roots **Sinhalese**

INGREDIENTS

2 tbsps white vinegar

1 tsp salt

1 tsp black pepper powder

2 tsps red chilli powder

1½ tbsps white sugar

2 raw or semi-ripe mangoes (600g), cut into 3cm cubes

As kids and even as adults, we would eat this pickle as a snack all the time. It's even better eaten as a bite with a beer or an arrack but is often eaten with rice and curry as well. Sweet, salty and sour, achcharu is such a cultural staple that it is often used as a reference in our day-to-day conversations; 'it was a real achcharu' which simply means, it was a real mix of everything. My mum often calls me an achcharu because of my mixed ethnic background.

Side note: any raw fruit—jambo, ripe pineapple, ambarella, olives, starfruit and guava—can be pickled using this method.

METHOD

1. In a bowl, mix all the ingredients together except for the mango; ensure that the sugar is all dissolved. Set aside for 5 minutes.

2. Add in the raw mango and mix well, ensuring every piece is well coated in the pickle paste. Let it marinate for 10–15 minutes before serving. Serve as a snack on its own or eat with rice and curry.

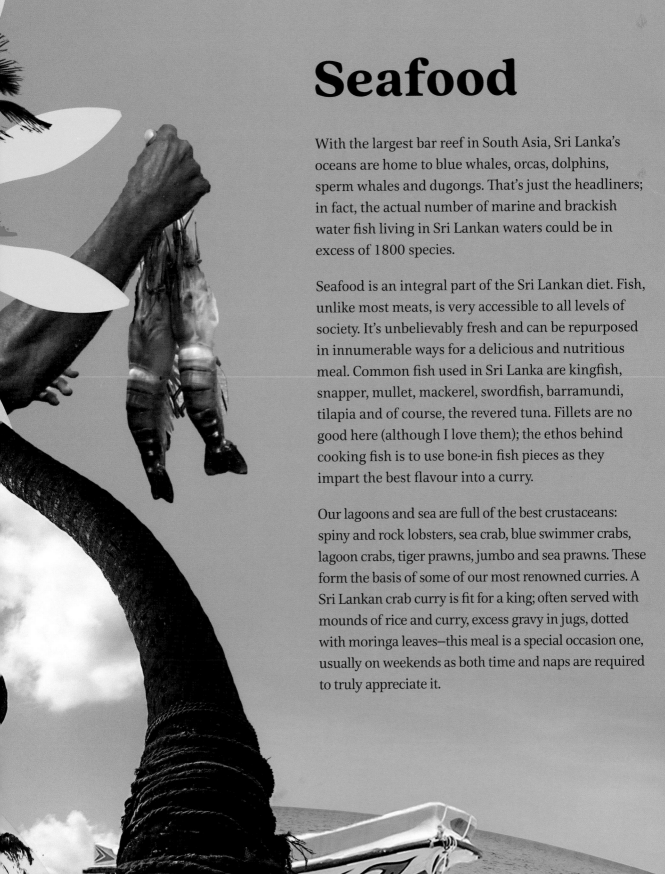

Seafood

With the largest bar reef in South Asia, Sri Lanka's oceans are home to blue whales, orcas, dolphins, sperm whales and dugongs. That's just the headliners; in fact, the actual number of marine and brackish water fish living in Sri Lankan waters could be in excess of 1800 species.

Seafood is an integral part of the Sri Lankan diet. Fish, unlike most meats, is very accessible to all levels of society. It's unbelievably fresh and can be repurposed in innumerable ways for a delicious and nutritious meal. Common fish used in Sri Lanka are kingfish, snapper, mullet, mackerel, swordfish, barramundi, tilapia and of course, the revered tuna. Fillets are no good here (although I love them); the ethos behind cooking fish is to use bone-in fish pieces as they impart the best flavour into a curry.

Our lagoons and sea are full of the best crustaceans: spiny and rock lobsters, sea crab, blue swimmer crabs, lagoon crabs, tiger prawns, jumbo and sea prawns. These form the basis of some of our most renowned curries. A Sri Lankan crab curry is fit for a king; often served with mounds of rice and curry, excess gravy in jugs, dotted with moringa leaves—this meal is a special occasion one, usually on weekends as both time and naps are required to truly appreciate it.

mirisata malu curry (chilli fish curry)

Serves **2-4** | Time **45 minutes** | Ethnic Roots **Sinhalese**

INGREDIENTS

Marinate for 30 mins

200g sail fish, cut into 2-inch cubes

1 tsp goraka paste/powder

½ tsp sea salt

1 tsp pepper

2 tsp red chilli powder

Pound in a pestle and mortar, or blitz in a food processor

2 garlic cloves

½ inch ginger (15g)

3 cardamoms

3 cloves

½ stick lemongrass

Have ready

3 tbsps sunflower or coconut oil

30g red onion, finely diced

10 curry leaves

3-inch piece pandan leaf (optional)

¼ tsp fenugreek seeds

2 fresh green chillies, minced

2 tsps roasted curry powder

480ml water

METHOD

1. In a deep saucepan, heat the coconut oil over a medium fire. Add the red onion, curry leaves, pandan leaf, fenugreek seeds, green chilli and caramelize. Cook for 3 minutes.

2. Mix in the pounded garlic-lemongrass spice mix and the marinated fish. Cook covered for 5 minutes.

3. Uncover, add in the roasted curry powder and mix well. Cook for 2 minutes before adding all the water.

4. Increase the heat and bring the water to the boil. Once the water is boiling (approximately 2 minutes), immediately turn it down, cover the pan and allow it to cook on a low heat for 15 minutes. If you want a redder, really spicy curry, after 5 minutes on a low heat, you can add another teaspoon of red chilli powder, mix it in and cook it on low for the rest of the allotted time. However, be warned this will be very fiery.

5. This curry will be runny after the low-heat, 15-minute cook. If you prefer a thicker gravy, cook uncovered for another 5–10 minutes till you get the consistency you prefer. Serve with rice, kiribath, roti or hoppers.

tinned fish curry

Serves **2-4** | Time **30 minutes** | Ethnic Roots **Multi-ethnic**

INGREDIENTS

For the gravy

1½ tbsps coconut oil or sunflower oil

3 shallots (50g), finely chopped

3 large garlic cloves, grated

30 grams ginger, grated

3-inch piece of lemongrass, roughly chopped

½ tsp mustard seeds

6 curry leaves

1½ tsps Jaffna curry powder

1 tsp turmeric powder

1 tsp chilli powder

1 tsp cumin powder

1 small tomato, chopped

1 tsp tamarind paste or concentrate

2 pieces goraka, soaked in ¼ cup of hot water

380ml water

120ml thick coconut milk

½ tsp salt

Keep ready

300g tinned sardines/ mackerel in oil or brine

Tinned and preserved fish is a popular item in Sri Lanka; used for cutlets, sambols and curries alike. In the UK, since tinned fish is not sold in large portions, I use small tins of sardines in oil and it produces a fabulous result. You can eat this with stringhoppers, dosas, crepes and even rice!

METHOD

1. In a small pan, heat the oil over a medium fire. Once the oil is hot, add in the shallots, and cook down for a few minutes. Add in the garlic, ginger, lemongrass, mustard seeds and curry leaves. Cook for a further 3–4 minutes until fragrant.

2. Add in the curry powder, turmeric powder, chilli powder, cumin powder, chopped tomato, tamarind paste and the goraka with its soaking water. Mix well. Add in the water and cook for 5 minutes before adding the coconut milk. Cook for 8–10 minutes until a thick gravy (hodi) is formed.

3. Mix in the sardines without the brine. Cook for a further 3–4 minutes. Finally, mix in the salt and combine well. Serve with pol roti or rice.

yellow fish curry

Serves **4** | Time **40 minutes** Ethnic Roots **Sinhalese**

INGREDIENTS

300g sail fish or white fish, diced into large cubes (2-inch cubes)

1½ tsps turmeric powder

1 tsp salt

8 curry leaves

2 tbsps coconut oil

1 whole red onion

3 cloves of garlic, finely diced

2 raw green chillies, chopped

3 goraka pieces soaked in 60ml hot water

2 tsps unroasted curry powder

1 tsp red chilli powder

100ml water

300ml thick coconut milk

METHOD

1. Marinate the washed fish with ½ teaspoon turmeric powder and ¼ tsp salt. Massage well into the fish and set aside.

2. In a large shallow pan on a medium-high heat, fry the curry leaves in 2 tablespoons of coconut oil. After 30 seconds, add in the chopped onions. Cook for 3 minutes or until the onion becomes tender. Add in the garlic and green chillies. Fry until the temper has wilted.

3. Add in the goraka along with its soaking water and the unroasted curry powder into the onion temper. After two minutes, if the temper starts to look a little dry, add about 3 tablespoons of water to make a thick paste. Add in the turmeric, red chilli powder and finally, the 100ml of water.

4. Drizzle in the coconut milk little by little, mixing constantly to make a thick gravy. Add the rest of the salt and mix well.

5. Immediately place the fish cubes carefully into the lightly boiling gravy and allow the fish to poach in the sauce. Turn the fish after two minutes, to ensure even cooking on all sides. The fish should cook fairly quickly, within 5–8 minutes at most. Turn off the heat. The heat from the gravy will continue cooking the fish, so it is important to ensure that it is delicately cooked through rather than overcooked.

6. Garnish the curry with chopped fresh coriander. Serve as part of a larger rice and curry meal, where the fish is the main protein.

Puttalam

The Puttalam region is iconic. It is said that Prince Vijaya (father of the Sinhalese race) first landed here from India with his 700 followers. A lot of my family hails from the northwestern province of the island, from Puttalam town itself. Their ancestral homes and culture are inextricably linked to this historic town. And the food of this area is unlike anything I have ever eaten before. Puttalam and seafood go hand in hand—they have every kind of curry ... stingray, catfish, lagoon fish, crab, prawn. They pride themselves on delicacies that you cannot get anywhere else in the country, like catfish egg omelettes and clam sambols.

My uncle Yaseen used to own a prawn farm in Puttalam back in the 1990s, a very popular farming product in that area; and when we were little, we used to go in time for the prawn harvest. They farmed a few varieties of prawns, so we would set up camp and all my cousins and I would go there to play, farm and eat the freshest prawns ever. After the harvest was done, everyone would cook a big meal, with the prawn curry being the star, and we would celebrate. Another reason Puttalam is famous is for its acres of salt pans; pink salt and table salt lend themselves to give extraordinary flavour to their curries.

The town is close to the national park called Wilpattu, which is one of the best places to see leopards, wild elephants and the most unusual flora and fauna. There is a baobab tree there (said to be brought over by Arab traders in the eleventh century) that they boast is almost 500 years old. On the outskirts of Wilpattu is an incredible set of mangroves (twenty-two of the overall twenty-seven varieties are in the region), and on the roots of these exquisite mangroves are metres and metres of wild oysters. Not just wild oysters, but crabs, spiny lobsters and clams! One of my favourite culinary adventures is to go collect wild oysters and eat them right on the boat! You'll never eat anything fresher.

cooked oysters with chilli, lime, coriander butter

Serves **2-4** | Prep **30 minutes** | Time **5 minutes**

INGREDIENTS

3 green chillies, roughly chopped

Juice of 1 lime

3 tbsps olive oil

150g coriander leaves and stems

200g butter, softened

1 tsp sea salt

10 fresh oysters

This is a very simple, quick-fire recipe; one that can be cooked on an open flame or even in the oven. If you can catch the oysters yourself, even better.

METHOD

1. In a food processor, blitz the green chillies, lime juice, olive oil, coriander leaves and stems till a green paste is formed. Add in the butter and salt, and blitz until a compound butter is formed. Wrap in clingfilm and roll into a sausage-like shape. Set aside in the fridge.

2. Clean and prep the oysters. Open them carefully.

3. Heat the grill function in the oven. Place the oysters in an ovenproof baking tray. You can secure the oysters by placing them on a mound of salt or in a foil ring. Add 1 tablespoon of butter to each oyster.

4. Transfer the oysters into the oven, directly under the grill. Cook them for 4–5 minutes until the butter has melted and infused into the oysters. Eat immediately, and be careful—the shells will be hot!

sri lankan crab curry

Serves **2-4** | Time **1 hour 20 minutes** | Ethnic Roots **Ceylon Tamil**

INGREDIENTS

Prepare, mix and marinate

1.5kg mud crab, cleaned and cut into pieces

1 tsp turmeric

½ tsp salt

Toast for 3 minutes over a medium heat and grind to a curry powder

2 tsps coriander seeds

2 tsps of cumin seed

1 tsp fennel seed

6 dried red chillies

2 tsp black pepper

1 cinnamon stick (5g), broken

1 tsp fenugreek seeds

1 tsp mustard seeds (optional)

Make a paste by grinding

20g garlic

20g ginger

100g onion, diced

200g tomato, deseeded/cored

1 stick lemongrass, chopped into 6 pieces

200g fresh grated coconut

If you are committed to cooking this cuisine, a Sri Lankan crab curry is a rite of passage. Every Lankan I know, loves it. Yes, it has a lot of ingredients, too many steps and the prep could be a whole Sunday morning affair, but master this and your friends will love you forever! The traditional way to serve this is to make lots of gravy (this naturally occurs when cooking crab because they release water and the shells season the curry) and have it on the side in jugs, so one can pour it all over their rice. The only other thing you may need to make is a pol sambol.

Have ready

4 tsps coconut oil

2 tsps tomato paste

10 curry leaves

2 tsps red chilli powder

150ml water

30g tamarind pieces dissolved in 100ml of water, seeds discarded

2 tsps Kashmiri red chilli powder

400ml coconut milk

1 tbsp sugar

1 tsp sea salt

100g moringa leaves

METHOD

1. Place a large saucepan or stockpot over a medium fire and heat the coconut oil. Add in the tomato paste and start to caramelize it. Fry for a minute before adding the ground onion, tomato and coconut paste. Cook for 2–3 minutes.

2. Next add in the curry leaves, chilli powder and mix. Cook for 2 minutes before adding the freshly ground curry powder. Incorporate into the temper and cook for a further 2 minutes. Splash in a little water (60ml) if it looks dry.

3. Add in the crab pieces and mix well. Cook for 5 minutes, then add the 150ml of water and the tamarind paste. Continue to cook covered for 10 minutes. The crab should turn to a bright fiery orange colour. Stir the crabs again, add 2 teaspoons of Kashmiri chilli powder, mix well and cook covered for another 5 minutes.

4. Stir the crab curry, and add the coconut milk, sugar and sea salt. Cook covered for another 3 minutes.

5. Uncover and cook for a further 5–10 minutes until a lovely medium-thick gravy is formed. Turn off the hob, add in the moringa leaves and mix well. Keep covered before serving. Perfect with fluffy white rice and lots of it! And a jug for all the additional crab gravy!

ambul thiyal

Serves **2-4** | Time **1 hour** | Ethnic Roots **Sinhalese**

INGREDIENTS

40g goraka

570ml water

1 tbsp whole peppercorns

4 cloves

20g garlic, peeled and left whole

5 cardamoms

500g tuna, washed, cleaned and cubed into large equal-sized pieces

1 heaped tsp salt

40 curry leaves

12 inches pandan leaves, torn into 6 pieces

1 cinnamon stick (5g)

2 fresh green chillies, sliced halfway

Another Sri Lankan banger, an ambul thiyal is a very dry, preserved curry but packs flavour. Tuna is essential for a good result; you can try meatier fishes but they won't be an ambul thiyal. For the best results, cook this dish in a clay pot. However, you can just as easily make this in a steel pot and produce an excellent result.

METHOD

1. In a small saucepan, on a high heat, boil the 40g goraka in 200ml of water for 10 minutes. The goraka is done when all the water has evaporated and the goraka pieces are soft.

2. In a food processor or a spice grinder, put the softened goraka, 70ml water, all the peppercorns, cloves, garlic and cardamoms. Blend till you have a thick aromatic black paste.

3. In a small bowl, mix the fish pieces with the goraka paste and salt, then massage well for 2 minutes, keeping the fish intact. Set aside.

4. In a deep saucepan, arrange half your curry leaves at the bottom of the pan, ensuring that there is a good level of leaves across it. Next, arrange the pandan leaves in a circle towards the edge of the pan.

5. Take each piece of fish and place it carefully in a circle on top of the curry leaves and pandan leaves, making sure that there is an empty circle in the middle of the fish. Mix 300 ml water with the remaining paste in the bowl, making a goraka gravy. Pour this gravy on the sides of the pan between the edge of the pan and the fish. Next, cover the fish with the rest of the curry leaves and start to turn the cubes of fish, rubbing the goraka gravy into each piece. Ensure that the position of the fish does not change.

6. Place the cinnamon stick in the centre and arrange the two chilli halves on the side of the pan on top of the fish. Cook covered over a medium heat for 30–40 minutes, turning the fish pieces every 10 minutes and shaking the pot at these intervals. You know this dish is done when a thick, aromatic black curry is formed.

cuttlefish curry

Serves **4** | Prep **1 hour** | Time **1 hour 10 minutes**

INGREDIENTS

300g cuttlefish, cut into strips

½ tsp turmeric paste/powder

25g tamarind, dissolved in 100ml hot water

1 tsp cracked black pepper

1 tsp salt

1½ tbsp roasted curry powder

1 tbsp chilli powder

1 tbsp coconut oil or sunflower oil

5 shallots, finely minced

2 garlic cloves (10g), finely minced

20 curry leaves

2 fresh green chillies, chopped

3x3-inch piece of pandan leaf

½ tsp fenugreek seeds

½ tsp mustard seeds

1 stick of lemongrass (10g), bashed

1 cinnamon quill (5g)

300ml thin coconut milk (150ml canned coconut milk, 150ml water)

METHOD

1. In a bowl, mix the cuttlefish, turmeric powder, tamarind water (with fruit), black pepper and the salt together. Allow the cuttlefish to marinate for 45 minutes.

2. In a small wok or frying pan, roast the curry powder and the chilli powder together over a high heat for 3 minutes. Immediately take off the heat and pour the spices into the cuttlefish, mixing well. Marinate for a further 15 minutes.

3. In a deep saucepan, heat the oil over a low heat. This curry should be cooked over a low fire. Once the oil has come to temperature, add the shallot, garlic, curry leaves, fresh chillies and pandan leaves. Fry for 2 minutes before adding the fenugreek seeds, mustard seeds, lemongrass and cinnamon quill. Fry for a further 5 minutes.

4. Add in the cuttlefish and fry for 5 minutes. Then place a lid over the pan and allow it to cook for another 5 minutes, stirring once or twice. Pour in 300ml of thin coconut milk and mix well. Cook covered for 45 minutes, stirring every few minutes. The end result should be a dark brown curry, and extremely tender cuttlefish.

kooniso curry (dried shrimp fry)

Serves **2-4** | Time **15 minutes** | Ethnic Roots **Multi-ethnic**

INGREDIENTS

2 tbsps neutral oil

120g red onion (¾ of an onion)

3 garlic cloves, chopped

20 curry leaves

2x3-inch pieces of pandan leaf

1 fresh green chilli, chopped into 3 pieces

½ tsp mustard seeds

½ cinnamon quill (2.5g)

60g dried shrimp, washed and drained

½ tsp salt

1 tbsp red chilli flakes

½ tsp turmeric powder/paste

½ tsp levelled black pepper powder

½ tomato, chopped into quarters

Juice of 1/2 a lime

In Sri Lanka, dried fish and shrimp are heavily consumed items. It's a little harder to find dried fish items globally but dried shrimp is more widely available, especially in East Asian supermarkets. If you don't fancy dried shrimp, then this dish works just as well with fresh baby shrimp or brown shrimp. Just make sure you spend a little more time cooking the fresh shrimp (at least 4–5 minutes longer).

METHOD

1. Place a frying pan over high heat and add the oil. Next, add the red onion, garlic cloves, curry leaves, pandan leaf pieces, green chilli, mustard seeds and cinnamon quill. Fry for 3 minutes, then add the dried prawns. Fry for 2 minutes, then mix in the salt, red chilli flakes and turmeric.

2. Fry for 1 minute, then add the pepper and tomato pieces and cook for a further 2 minutes. Take off the heat and add the juice of half a lime. Mix well and serve.

prawn curry

Serves **2-4** | Prep **30 minutes** | Time **30 minutes**

INGREDIENTS

For the prawn stock:

½ tsp salt

1 tsp baking soda

1 tbsp coconut oil or neutral oil

500g jumbo prawns, shells and heads on

1 tbsp tomato paste

75g red onion, roughly chopped

3 cloves garlic, roughly chopped

1 tbsp coriander seeds

1 tbsp cumin seeds

500ml water

For the curry:

2 tbsps coconut oil or neutral oil

1 tsp salt

1 red onion (100g), diced

1 large stalk lemongrass, pounded and cut into 3 pieces

8–10 curry leaves

3 inches of pandan leaf, torn into 3 parts

30g garlic paste

30g ginger paste

1 tsp mustard seeds

2 tsps red chilli powder

½ tsp turmeric paste or powder

1½ tsp unroasted curry powder

200ml thick coconut milk

A handful of moringa leaves (optional)

This is a simple curry and relies very heavily on a good, punchy stock as its base. Using jumbo prawns instead of medium-sized ones makes this a showstopper.

METHOD

1. Peel and devein the prawns. Remove the heads and shells but keep a small part of the shell on the tails. Set the shells and heads aside for stock. You can keep two prawns with heads on for presentation if you want. Wash the prawns, dry and place in a bowl. To the deshelled prawns, add ½ teaspoon of salt and the baking soda and mix well. Let them brine for 10–15 minutes.

2. In a saucepan or stockpot, heat 1 tablespoon of oil over a medium fire. Sauté the prawn shells and heads; cook for 2 minutes or until they start to turn pink. Mix in the tomato paste and cook for 2 minutes before adding in the onions, garlic, coriander seeds and cumin seeds. Fry for at least 3 minutes and until fragrant and the shells have started to lightly brown. Add in 500ml of water and cook for 15 mins over medium heat. The stock should have reduced by half and be a dark red-brown colour; you should be left with at least 250ml of stock. Drain through a fine sieve to remove spices and shells.

3. In a saucepan, heat 2 tablespoons oil over a medium-high heat. Add in the red onion, lemongrass, curry leaves, and pandan leaves. Cook for 2–3 minutes until the onions start to sweat. Add in the garlic paste, ginger paste and the mustard seeds. Cook for 2 minutes.

4. Next, add the red chilli powder, turmeric paste and unroasted curry powder. Mix into the temper and sauté for another 2 to 3 minutes. Stir in the prawn stock and cook for 4 minutes before adding in the thick coconut milk and salt. Mix well and reduce for 3 minutes.

5. Add in the raw prawns. Cook all the prawns on one side for 2–3 minutes each and then turn over and repeat, till they turn bright orange. Take the curry off the heat and garnish with moringa leaves. Allow it to sit for 3–4 minutes before serving. Serve immediately with rice, stringhoppers, hoppers, pittu or roti.

Vegetables

Sri Lanka has lots of weird and wonderful vegetables; knobbly, unusual, and sometimes wholly unique to the island, vegetables are a mainstay of Lankan cuisine. You simply cannot have a meal without at least two vegetable curry preparations. This is the core reason why it is so easy and delicious to follow a vegetarian diet in the country.

There are so many different types of vegetables and multiple ways to eat each one. Some of my favourites include bittergourd (better known as bitter melon), snakegourd, moringa sticks, lotus root, gotukola leaves and sarana leaves.

A majority of Sri Lankan cuisine is vegan—we tend to avoid dairy in our curries and the base for most are water or coconut milk. To become a seasoned pro at Sri Lankan food one must master the coconut; understand what milk extraction is needed for each cooking stage, how to break and grate the coconut and of course, how to pick the correct coconut.

This is one of my favourite sections of the book; you will note that the vegetable is the hero of the dish, and imparts the majority of the flavour to the curry. If you are a more confident cook, able to multitask, you can have three vegetable dishes prepped, cooked and on the table in 30 to 40 minutes.

garlic curry

Serves **4** | Time **50 minutes** | Ethnic Roots **Ceylon Tamil**

INGREDIENTS

For the curry powder:

3 tbsp fresh grated or desiccated coconut

2 tbsps whole black peppercorns

1 tsp mustard seeds

1 tsp fenugreek seeds

6 cloves

1 tbsp chilli powder

For the gravy:

1 tbsp tamarind paste/syrup

400ml thick tinned coconut milk

2 tbsps coconut oil

½ red onion, finely diced

6 curry leaves

2 fresh green chillies, finely diced

200g large cloves garlic, peeled and left whole

120ml water

1 teaspoon turmeric powder/ paste

1 tsp white sugar

1½ tsps salt

This could be seen as a very brave curry to eat (especially if you are planning a date night!) but rest assured that cooking gets rid of the garlic's 'pungent' odour. Even though peeling all of the garlic cloves takes a lot of time, there are amazing hacks on the internet that can cut the time for this task. Give it a go, and you won't be disappointed. Pair with yellow rice and red chicken curry.

METHOD

1. On a high heat, in a shallow non-stick frying pan, dry roast the coconut for 3 minutes until it turns golden to dark brown. Set aside. Next, dry roast the peppercorns for 2 minutes and set aside. Then dry roast the mustard seeds, the fenugreek seeds and cloves for 1–2 minutes and set aside. Finally, dry roast the chilli powder for 1–1.5 minutes, until it turns a dark brick red colour. Immediately take off the heat and grind all the dry spices with the roast coconut to a fine powder.

2. Add in the tamarind paste to half the coconut milk and mix well. Set aside.

3. In a deep saucepan, heat the coconut oil and add in the onions, curry leaves and green chillies. Fry until aromas are released and the onion starts to caramelize (approx. 3 minutes).

4. Next, add in half of the freshly ground powder and combine well. If it looks like the temper is burning, add a little water (approx. 60ml).

5. To this spiced temper, add in the garlic cloves and cook for 4–5 minutes. Add the remaining ground spices, the turmeric, the rest of the water and mix carefully taking care to not bruise the garlic cloves. Cook for 5 minutes before adding in the prepared tamarind-coconut milk. Cook for a further 5 minutes, stirring well before covering with a lid. Cook on a low to medium heat for a further 10 minutes.

6. A thick, dark gravy should form. Uncover and add in the remaining 200ml of coconut milk, the sugar and the salt. Mix well and ensure the cloves are still whole before covering and cooking on low to medium for another 10 minutes. After the final cook, the curry should be a rich, dark colour, punchy in flavour and the cloves should be tender but not falling apart.

my garden moringa mallung

Serves **4** | Time **15 minutes** | Ethnic Roots **Sinhalese**

INGREDIENTS

150g moringa (drumstick) leaves, removed from stems and finely chopped

50g shallot, finely diced

40g freshly grated coconut

1 fresh green chilli, finely diced

¼ tsp turmeric powder

½ tsp salt

Mallungs are a style of cooked leaf preparation. Packed with nutrients like Vitamin A, B1, magnesium, calcium, potassium, iron and zinc—moringa is a superfood. Widely eaten across Sri Lanka, it is often served as a mallung as the leaves are too bitter to eat raw. Moringa is native to the country, and a lucky few like me have a tree growing in their garden! Winning.

METHOD

1. In a big bowl, mix all the ingredients together, ensuring that the moringa leaves are mixed well with the shallot, coconut and chilli.

2. Heat a frying pan over a high heat, and add the leaf mixture and cook whilst stirring for 3 minutes. Immediately take off the heat and continue to mix for another minute. Serve with rice and curry!

sautéed beet leaves

Serves **4** | Time **10 minutes** | Ethnic Roots **Multi-ethnic**

INGREDIENTS

1 tbsp coconut oil

75g red onion, thinly sliced

3 garlic cloves, thinly sliced

2 green chillies, cut diagonally

250g beetroot leaves, washed and leaves left whole, stems diced

½ tsp red chilli powder

½ tsp turmeric powder

1 tsp salt

Never, ever, throw away those beetroot tops. A great source of iron and calcium, the leaves are delicious, packed with nutrition and super yummy when cooked as a mallung.

METHOD

1. In a frying pan, heat the coconut oil over a medium flame. Add the red onion, garlic and green chillies. Sauté for 1 minute before adding in the beet leaves and stems. Temper for further 2 minutes.

2. Add in the red chilli powder, turmeric powder, salt and mix well. Sauté for a 2–3 minutes. The dish is ready when the leaves have softened and turned a dark green and the onions and garlic will also have turned pink. Serve with rice and curry.

leek fry

Serves **4** | Time **20 minutes** | Ethnic Roots **Sinhalese**

INGREDIENTS

2 tbsps coconut oil or ghee

½ red onion, diced into small cubes

20g garlic paste

20g ginger paste

1 fresh green chilli, finely diced

250g leeks, cut into rounds, approximately 1cm thick in width

1 tsp turmeric

½ tsp mustard seeds

1½ tsps chilli flakes

½ tsp salt

METHOD

1. Take a frying pan and put over a medium heat. Add in the oil and heat. Next, add the red onion and cook for 3 minutes until the onion starts to soften and turns translucent.

2. Mix in the garlic paste, ginger paste and diced fresh green chilli. Fry till the onion starts to caramelize, approximately 3 minutes.

3. Add the leeks and cook down. Once the leeks start to soften, mix in the turmeric, mustard seeds and chilli flakes. Cook down for a few minutes, but ensure that the leeks retain their vibrant green colour.

4. After 4 minutes, add in the salt and combine well. Serve piping hot with rice and curry!

ala thel dhala (chilli fried potatoes)

Serves **4** | Time **45 minutes** | Ethnic Roots **Sinhalese**

INGREDIENTS

450g potatoes, peeled and cut into equal-sized cubes (4cm)

1 tsp turmeric powder

1 tsp salt

2 tsps maldive fish, pounded and ground to a powder (omit for vegetarians)

3 tbsps ghee

6 curry leaves

2 fresh green chillies, finely chopped

1 large banana shallot/ 2 shallots, finely chopped lengthwise

3 large garlic cloves, minced

½ tsp raw red chilli powder

1 tbsp dried chilli flakes

Not the most authentic version of this dish—most recipes would never fry the potatoes separately; however, I love a good crispy tattie and I think it gives the dish a big flavour boost as well as texture. If you want to be authentic, boil the potatoes fully in step 1 and skip step 3 altogether.

Tips: A Yukon potato works best because it is semi-waxy and semi-starchy in form. Waxy potatoes like new potatoes or charlotte potatoes are the next best alternative.

A good substitute for maldive fish is bonito flakes. This is the umami element that Sri Lankans always add to their dishes for that final boost of flavour.

If you do not have ghee, it would be advisable to use a non-fragrant oil for frying the potatoes. Use butter when you are cooking the onion temper instead of oil.

METHOD

1. Parboil the potatoes with ½ teaspoon of turmeric powder and ½ teaspoon salt. Drain and set aside to cool. This will lend the potato its iconic yellow colour.

2. Grind the maldive fish and ½ teaspoon salt together to make a seasoned salt. Set aside for finishing later.

3. Prepare all the ingredients as the recipe requires the cook to work fast. Take a wide non-stick frying pan and set it over a medium-high heat. Add 1 tablespoon ghee and when it is hot, immediately add in the potato cubes (this might have to be done in batches). Fry the potatoes, turning them constantly till crispy. Do not overcook at this stage. Remove the potatoes and set aside.

4. Return the frying pan back to a medium-high flame, and put in 1 tablespoon ghee. Once the ghee is heated, add in the curry leaves, green chillies and allow to cook for 30 seconds to 1 minute. Add in the shallots and garlic, cook till they start to sweat and caramelize.

5. Toss in the chilli powder, dried chilli flakes, ½ teaspoon turmeric powder, 1 tablespoon ghee and fry for 1 minute, mixing well.

6. Immediately add the fried potato cubes and mix quickly. Ensure the potatoes are well coated in the chilli flake mixture.

7. Finally, sprinkle the maldive fish salt over the potatoes. The potatoes should start to take on a golden yellow colour from the spices. Cook for at least 5 minutes.

8. Remove from heat and garnish with fresh coriander leaves if you want a little punch of freshness, and serve with rice.

The Pola

Saturdays at the 'pola' (Sinhalese for market) were a ritual for my mother and I. And ours is the Colpetty market, which was constructed in the 1970s and was inspired by Le Corbusier's Villa Savoye. Walking past the colourful isles of fresh produce, the fish and meat floor run by a mafia of cats and the incredible imported food stalls upstairs, it was my version of wonderland as a child.

In its current dishevelled state, it is no longer an attractive option for many. But it remains my favourite as one of Colombo's few places where you can get (almost) all your ingredients.

Purchasing from anyone other than 'our vegetable guy' or 'our fruit guy' was as scandalous as cheating on your partner. Our vegetable stall here is Beemaah's. It was my grandparents' vegetable stall and is mine today. Beemaah's is run by the extremely entrepreneurial Ashraff, who inherited the business from his father. Dressed in his characteristic uniform of a clean pressed shirt and sarong, this unassuming man always has a keen eye trained on his stall. What few people know is that he's one of the largest vegetable distributors in the country, catering to the biggest hotel chains, restaurants, plus a strong client base of expats. Once, I overheard him speak perfect Mandarin to a Chinese client. Blown away, I asked him about it. Ashraff revealed that he learnt seven languages, and even more incredibly, taught them to his staff, so they can sell to expats in Sri Lanka. If you want to learn real entrepreneurship, a conversation with Ashraff and ten minutes of watching his staff will do.

pineapple curry

Serves **4** | Time **35 minutes** | Ethnic Roots **Ceylon Moors**

INGREDIENTS

3 tbsps coconut oil

1 red onion, finely diced

2 whole star anise

1 cinnamon quill

2 tsps mustard seeds

6 cloves

12 curry leaves

4 cloves garlic, finely minced

30g ginger, finely grated

2 fresh green bird's eye chillies, finely minced

½ tsp roasted curry powder

1 tbsp chilli powder

1 tsp turmeric powder

1 whole peeled pineapple, chopped into equal-sized cubes

240ml water

240ml tinned coconut milk

1 tbsp white sugar

1 tsp salt

Lankans love a good fruit curry. Even though the star ingredient is fruit, this is considered a 'vegetarian' curry as it is served as a savoury side dish. Pineapple curry and biryani go hand in hand, especially in Muslim communities in Sri Lanka. Sweet but tart, this is an excellent preparation if you are looking for a different kind of 'veg' curry.

METHOD

1. Warm the oil in a deep pan, over a medium heat. Add the red onion, star anise, cinnamon, mustard seeds, cloves and curry leaves. Cook for 3 minutes until fragrant and the onion starts to wilt. Add the garlic, ginger and fresh green chillies. Fry till the onion starts to caramelize, approximately 2 minutes.

2. Add in the curry powder and mix well. Sprinkle in the chilli powder and turmeric. Splash in a little water and mix well if the temper gets too dry.

3. Toss in the pineapple cubes and mix well. Add in the water and cook for about 5 minutes. The pineapple will start to release its own juices and make a syrup-like gravy.

4. Stir in the coconut milk and simmer for 10 minutes or until the gravy thickens (consistency should be similar to single cream). Finally, add the sugar and salt into the curry. Take off the heat after 3 minutes and allow it to rest for 10–15 minutes before serving.

Tips: To avoid getting pieces of spices in your meals, get a piece of muslin and put all the star anise, cinnamon, cloves in it and wrap it tightly. Bash it lightly with the back of a knife or a pestle to release its aromas and drop it in the pan with the rest of the ingredients. Before you serve the dish, pull out the muslin parcel and be bit-free!

fried okra curry

Serves **2-4** | Time **40 minutes** | Ethnic Roots **Indian Tamil**

INGREDIENTS

To prepare the okra for frying:

100g okra

¼ tsp turmeric powder

½ tsp salt

150ml coconut oil

For the curry:

20g tamarind (½ tsp tamarind concentrate)

200ml thick coconut milk

60ml cup water

2 tbsps coconut oil

50g red onion, diced finely

20g garlic cloves, chopped

¼ tsp fenugreek seeds

1 inch pandan leaf, torn

6 curry leaves

¼ tsp turmeric powder

1 tsp unroasted curry powder

½ tsp salt (optional)

1½ tsp chilli flakes

¼ tsp chilli powder

1 tsp brown sugar

A departure from the usual okra fry, this Tamil curry is slightly sweet, salty and jammy! It's a crowd pleaser because not only is it fried, but it is cooked down in coconut milk giving it a unique flavour.

METHOD

1. Mix the okra, turmeric powder and salt in a small bowl and marinate for 5 minutes. Heat the oil in a small hopper pan or saucepan and fry the okra pieces in batches. Each batch needs to fry over medium heat for at least 5 minutes, or until the edges of the okra starts to brown. Drain the okra on paper towels to get rid of any excess oil.

2. Mix the tamarind with the coconut milk and 60ml water. Leave for 10 minutes; the coconut milk should be light brown in colour. Strain the tamarind seeds. If using concentrate, just mix well.

3. Next, in a small frying pan, heat about 2 tablespoons of coconut oil over medium heat. Add in the onions and cook for 3 minutes. Then, add in the garlic, fenugreek seeds, pandan and curry leaves. Immediately turn the fire down to a very low heat and continue to cook for at least 5 minutes.

4. Add in the turmeric powder, okra, curry powder, salt and mix well. Cook for 2 minutes before adding the chilli flakes, chilli powder and brown sugar. Mix well and cook for a further 4 minutes, before adding the tamarind-infused coconut milk to the curry. Cook down for at least 8 minutes or until most of the coconut milk has been absorbed and you are left with a thick, jammy curry.

my dad's tharaka dhal (lentil curry)

Serves **2-4** | Time **50 minutes** | Ethnic Roots **Multi-ethnic**

INGREDIENTS

260g red split lentils

720ml water

1 tbsp turmeric powder

1 fresh green chilli, sliced lengthwise

1-inch piece fresh ginger (grated)

1 medium tomato, chopped into small cubes

120ml tinned coconut milk

1 tbsp vegetable/ sunflower oil

½ red onion (finely diced)

2 cloves garlic, finely sliced

2 dried whole red chillies (optional)

2 tsps mustard seeds

200g baby leaf spinach

Sea salt to taste

On a trip to London when I was eleven, my father showed me how to make this dish. This is also a recipe he taught my mom when they first got married, and one that he would often cook when he lived in England about thirty years prior. Since then, I've put my own spin on it and tried making it a little healthier by adding in baby leaf spinach.

METHOD

1. Wash the lentils under cold running water, till the water runs clean. Boil the lentils in a medium-sized pan over a medium heat with all of the water, turmeric, fresh chilli, ginger and tomato. Once the lentils come to a rigorous boil, reduce the heat to a low fire and allow it to simmer. Stir occasionally to ensure the turmeric is well combined and the tomatoes melt into the dhal.

2. After about 20 minutes, some of the water should have evaporated, and the dhal should resemble the consistency of a thick soup, the lentils mushy to touch. At this point stir in the coconut milk and cook for a further 5–10 minutes.

3. In a separate frying pan, heat the oil on a high fire. Fry the onions, garlic and dried whole chillies until the onions caramelize. Then add the mustard seeds and fry for 3 minutes. Set aside.

4. Set the dhal on a low heat and add the fragrant temper into it. Mix well to ensure that the temper is evenly spread throughout the lentils.

5. Place all the spinach on top of the dhal and allow it to steam and wilt into the dhal. Give it one last mix and add the salt to taste. Turn off the heat and serve.

Tip: If you don't have tinned coconut milk, cow's milk is a great substitute—you'll get a great result at the end!

thalana batu (thai eggplant curry)

Serves **2-4** | Time **30 minutes** | Ethnic Roots **Sinhalese**

INGREDIENTS

200g thalana batu, halved and deseeded

1 tsp curry powder

1 tsp chilli powder

½ tsp turmeric powder

½ tsp sea salt

2 tbsps coconut oil

50g red onion, chopped finely

5g cinnamon stick or half a quill

3 cloves garlic, minced

6 curry leaves

6-inch piece of pandan leaf, torn

¼ tsp fenugreek seeds

¼ tsp mustard seeds

1 fresh green chilli, chopped

120ml thin coconut milk (60ml canned coconut milk, 60ml water)

120ml thick coconut milk

Thalana batu, also known as Thai eggplant, is a wonderful vegetable that I have seen available in many Asian supermarkets. This super vegetable is used in natural medicine, hailed to treat heart disease, asthma, body aches and fever.

METHOD

1. In a bowl, mix the cleaned thalana batu, curry powder, chilli powder, turmeric powder, salt and set aside.

2. Heat a saucepan over a medium fire and pour in the oil. Once hot, add in the red onion, cinnamon stick, garlic, curry leaves, pandan leaf, fenugreek seeds, mustard seeds and green chilli and fry for 4 minutes.

3. Add in the marinated thalana batu and fry for 2 minutes. Reduce the heat to low, add in the thin coconut milk and cook covered for 10 minutes.

4. Add in the thick coconut milk and cook covered for another 5 minutes. Remove the lid and cook for 3–5 minutes, or until the gravy thickens.

tomato curry

Serves **2-4** | Time **35 minutes** | Ethnic Roots **Ceylon Moor/Multi-ethnic**

INGREDIENTS

3 pieces tamarind, soaked in hot water (30ml)
or 1 tbsp tamarind paste

1 tbsp coconut oil

50g red onion, chopped

2 fresh red bird's eye chillies, chopped

½ tsp fenugreek seeds

12–16 curry leaves

1 tbsp garlic paste

1 tbsp ginger paste

3 tbsps tomato paste

3 large tomatoes (200g–250g), blanched, with skins removed, chopped into fairly large chunks

2 tsps coriander powder

1 tsp turmeric powder

½ of a whole lime pickle (20g), minced

120ml water

1 tsp white sugar

240ml thick coconut milk

METHOD

1. Soak the tamarind in hot water for at least 10 minutes. Reserve the water and the fruit, discard the seeds. Mash into a rough paste. Set aside.

2. Heat the coconut oil in a saucepan, over a medium heat. Once hot, add in the onion, red chillies, fenugreek seeds and curry leaves. Temper for 2 minutes before adding in the garlic paste, ginger paste and the tomato paste. Cook the tomato paste, mixing well, for 2–3 minutes.

3. Add in the chopped tomatoes and quickly follow with the coriander powder, turmeric powder and the minced lime pickle. Cook for 3–4 minutes before adding the water, white sugar and the tamarind paste. Cook covered for 5 minutes.

4. Tip in the coconut milk and cook for 10 minutes on a low heat. A thick, bright red tomato gravy should be formed. The tomato pieces tend to disintegrate. Serve with rice or stringhoppers.

brinjal moju

Serves **2-4** | Time **25 minutes** | Ethnic Roots **Ceylon Tamil**

INGREDIENTS

240ml coconut oil, reserve 2 tbsps oil for frying

2 large eggplants or 5 brinjals, cut into 7cm x 2cm batons

10 whole small shallots, skins peeled, left whole

6 fresh green chillies, stalks removed, left whole

10 curry leaves

30g ginger paste

30g garlic paste

2 tsps roast curry powder

2 tsps flakes red chillies

1 tbsp white sugar

2 tbsps white vinegar

1 tsp table or sea salt

METHOD

1. In a small saucepot or a small wok, heat the 200ml of coconut oil over a medium heat. Once the oil is hot, start frying the eggplant batons in batches, making sure they are golden brown (approximately 4–5 minutes a batch). Once all the eggplant batons are fried, set aside and drain on some paper. Next, fry the peeled shallots whole in the same oil for 1–1½ minutes. Drain on paper towels and set aside. Repeat for the whole fresh green chillies. Drain on paper towels and set aside.

2. Heat a small wok or non-stick frying pan over a medium fire. Once the pan is hot, add the reserved coconut oil and bring to temperature. Add the curry leaves, temper for 1 minute before adding in the garlic and ginger pastes. Sauté for 2 minutes before adding in the roast curry powder and fry for another 1 minute. Immediately, add in the red chilli flakes, the white sugar and the white vinegar and cook for 3 minutes, until a thickish brown sauce is formed and the sugar has dissolved.

3. Next add in the fried eggplant batons, salt, fried green chillies, fried shallots and mix well into the curry paste/sauce and cook for 3–4 minutes. The final dish should be dark brown in colour and a dry, thick curry with little or no gravy, similar to a chutney.

tempered beetroot fry

Serves **2-4** | Time **25 minutes** | Ethnic Roots **Sinhalese**

INGREDIENTS

250g beetroot, peeled, julienned into ½cm x 5cm pieces

½ tsp salt

¼ tsp ground black pepper

¼ tsp turmeric powder/paste

1 tbsp coconut oil

25g red onion, sliced into half moons

20 curry leaves

2 x 3-inch (7cm) pieces of pandan leaf

4 garlic cloves (20g), chopped

½ tsp fenugreek seeds

½ tsp mustard seeds

½ cinnamon quill

2 fresh green chillies, chopped into large pieces

4 tbsps water

1 levelled tbsp red chilli flakes

METHOD

1. In a bowl, mix the beetroot, salt, pepper and turmeric together. Set aside.

2. Heat the coconut oil in a frying pan over medium fire. Add the red onion, curry leaves, pandan leaves, garlic, fenugreek seeds, mustard seeds, cinnamon quill and fresh green chillies. Temper for 3 minutes.

3. Mix in the seasoned beetroot, and fry for 3 minutes before adding water and covering with a lid. Cook for 10 minutes, stirring every couple of minutes.

4. Add in the red chilli flakes and fry for 3 minutes, stirring rigorously to make sure that the chilli flakes are mixed through. Serve with yellow or white rice.

One of Sri Lanka's most famous dishes, everyone knows a Sri Lankan beetroot curry. What a lot of people don't know is that there are a number of different preparations of beetroot we make. From a tempered fry to salads and mallungs, there are a variety of ways to enjoy this humble vegetable.

polos curry (jackfruit curry)

Serves **2-4** | Time **1 hour 40 minutes** | Ethnic Roots **Sinhalese**

INGREDIENTS

For the curry powder:

15 dried red chillies

15 cloves

6 cardamoms

1 cinnamon quill (5g)

1 levelled tsp pepper

2 levelled tbsps coriander seeds

1 levelled tbsp cumin seeds

For the rest of the curry:

½ tsp turmeric powder/ paste

2 tsps salt

500g young jackfruit, cleaned and cut into large equal-sized pieces

2 tbsps coconut oil

50g red onion (½ onion), cut as half moons

4 large garlic cloves (30g), chopped

8g goraka fruit

2 fresh green chillies, chopped into large pieces

4x7cm piece of pandan leaf

20 curry leaves (5g)

½ tsp fenugreek seeds

½ tsp mustard seeds

500ml thin coconut milk (250ml canned coconut milk, 250ml water mix)

530ml thick coconut milk

If you can, cook this dish in a clay pot. Doing so adds a flavour dimension to this preparation that is out of this world.

METHOD

1. Heat a frying pan over a high fire, and roast the curry powder ingredients for 3–4 minutes. Once browned, remove the spices from the heat immediately and set aside. Cool for a few minutes and grind into a fine powder. Set aside.

2. Combine the turmeric, 1 teaspoon salt and the young jackfruit pieces in a bowl, making sure to coat each piece thoroughly. Set aside.

3. In a deep saucepan, heat the coconut oil over a medium heat. Add the onion, chopped garlic, goraka, fresh green chillies, pandan leaves, curry leaves and fry for 3–4 minutes. Stir in the fenugreek and mustard seeds, and fry for another 2 minutes.

4. Mix in the seasoned young jackfruit, and fry for 4 minutes, making sure to brown it on all sides. Add in 4 heaped tsps curry powder (reserve the spare for later) and fry further for 3 minutes. Stir in the thin coconut milk. Cover and cook for 5 minutes, then tip in ¾ of the thick coconut milk and stir well.

5. Allow the curry to come to the boil (approximately 5–7 minutes), then turn down the heat to low and cook covered for 20 minutes, stirring occasionally. Stir in 180ml thick coconut milk and cook for 30 minutes on low with the lid covered. Add in 2 heaped teaspoons of the curry powder, 1 teaspoon of salt and mix well. Cook covered for another 10 minutes on low until you have a reduced, thick, dark brown curry.

raw mango curry

Serves **2-4** | Time **1 hour** | Ethnic Roots **Ceylon Tamil/Indian Tamil**

INGREDIENTS

Grind into a paste using a food processor or spice grinder:

20g ginger

4 cloves garlic (20g)

5 cardamoms

10 cloves

For the curry:

300g raw mango, cut into quarters

1 tsp salt

¼ tsp turmeric powder/paste

2 tbsps coconut oil

50–60g red onion

2 fresh green chillies

10 curry leaves

3x7cm pieces of pandan leaf

1 stick of lemongrass (10g)

½ tsp fenugreek seeds

½ tsp mustard seeds

1 tsp unroasted curry powder

1 cinnamon quill (5g)

2 tsps red chilli powder

240ml canned coconut milk

240ml water

100g jaggery, grated

2 tsps roasted curry powder

METHOD

1. In a bowl, mix the mango, salt and turmeric powder together. Set aside.

2. In a medium-sized saucepan, heat the coconut oil over a medium heat. Add the onion, garlic-ginger paste, fresh green chillies, curry leaves, pandan leaves and the lemongrass. Fry for 3 minutes before adding the fenugreek and mustard seeds. Add the seasoned mango and fry for another 4 minutes. Add in the unroasted curry powder, cinnamon, chilli powder and mix well. Fry for another 3–4 minutes, till the mango is starting to lightly brown and the spices are roasted. Stir in the coconut milk and the water, reduce the heat to medium-low and cook covered for 15 minutes.

3. Stir in the jaggery and cook covered for 5 minutes. Add in the roasted curry powder and mix well. Cook covered for 10 minutes on a low heat and then remove lid and cook for another 10 minutes. The result should be a thick and dark-coloured curry and the raw mango should be tender and cooked through.

white pumpkin curry

Serves **2-4** | Time **40 minutes** | Ethnic Roots **Sinhalese**

INGREDIENTS

Grind into a smooth paste using a food processor or spice grinder:

3 garlic cloves, chopped

½ tsp mustard seeds

½ tsp whole black peppercorns

25g fresh grated coconut

60ml water (¼ cup)

For the curry:

400g pumpkin, cut into large equal-sized pieces

1 tsp turmeric paste/ powder

1½ tsps salt

1 tbsp coconut oil

50g–75g red onion, cut in half moons

2 cloves of garlic, chopped

½ tsp fenugreek seeds

1 cinnamon quill (5g)

15 curry leaves

3x7cm pandan leaves

1 tsp unroasted curry powder

200ml thin coconut milk

250ml thick coconut milk

METHOD

1. In a bowl, add the pumpkin, ½ teaspoon of turmeric powder, salt. Mix and marinate for 5 minutes.

2. In a deep saucepan, heat the oil over a medium fire. Add in the red onion, the chopped garlic, fenugreek seeds, cinnamon quill, curry leaves, pandan leaves and fry for 5 minutes. Mix in the pumpkin pieces, unroasted curry powder, ½ teaspoon turmeric powder and fry for 5 minutes, until the pumpkin starts to brown. Pour in the thin coconut milk and cook covered for 5 minutes, stirring occasionally. Cook uncovered for 5 minutes.

3. In another bowl, mix the thick coconut milk with the ground mustard-coconut paste. Lower the heat, and add in the mustard-coconut milk into the pumpkin. Constantly stir for 8–10 minutes and remove from the heat. Serve with rice.

cashew curry

Serves **4** | Time **1 hour** | Ethnic Roots **Sinhalese**

INGREDIENTS

150g raw cashew; most of them should be split

200ml water

75g red onion, chopped

15g garlic, minced

1 tbsp coconut oil (heaped)

¼ tsp fenugreek seeds

½ tsp cumin seeds

5g cinnamon sticks (½ quill)

10 curry leaves

1 piece pandan leaf

4 cloves

2 tbsps unroasted curry powder

½ tsp turmeric powder

1 tsp red chilli powder

300ml thin coconut milk (if using a can, 100ml thick coconut milk and 200ml water)

1 tsp white sugar

200ml thick coconut milk

100g frozen peas or petit pois

2 tsps salt

METHOD

1. In a bowl, soak the raw cashew with 200ml of room temperature water for at least 30 minutes. If possible, soak for 1–1 1/2 hours. Strain and set aside.

2. In a medium saucepan, over a medium-high heat, bring the coconut oil to temperature. Then add the fenugreek seeds, cumin seeds, curry leaves, pandan leaves, cinnamon stick, cloves and fry for 3–4 minutes. Next, add in the onion and start to soften and sweat them. After a further 3–4 minutes, add in the garlic and fry for 2–3 minutes until, they start to cook down but not brown.

3. Once the onion temper is slightly caramelized and soften, add in the soaked cashew nuts and sauté for at least 2 minutes before adding in the unroasted curry powder, turmeric and chilli powder. Mix well (ensuring the cashew stays intact) with 1 teaspoon of salt and cook for a further 2 minutes. If any point cashews are starting to catch to the pan, add 60–100ml of water.

4. Next add in the additional the thin coconut milk and cook covered for 10–15 minutes until a rich spiced aroma has formed, and the cashews have a thin 'gravy'.

5. Once a curry has started to take shape, add in the sugar, and 200ml thick coconut milk and cook covered for another 10 minutes. Add the frozen garden peas and then cook uncovered for at least an additional 5 minutes. Finally add the last teaspoon of salt and cook for 3 minutes until a semi-thick gravy has formed. The cashews should taste soft but al dente to give a bit of texture to the curry.

pathola (snakegourd) curry

Serves **2-4** | Time **30 minutes** | Ethnic Roots **Sinhalese**

INGREDIENTS

300g snakegourd, peeled, cleaned and chopped into 2-inch pieces

¼ tsp fenugreek seeds

½ tsp turmeric powder

1 tsp unroasted curry powder

½ cinnamon quill

¼ tsp black pepper

240ml thin coconut milk

¼ tsp mustard seeds

240ml thick coconut milk

METHOD

1. In a saucepan, mix the snakegourd, fenugreek seeds, ¼ teaspoon of turmeric powder, unroasted curry powder, cinnamon quill, black pepper and thin coconut milk. Cook covered for 15 minutes, over medium fire.

2. In a pestle and mortar, pound the mustard seeds and ¼ teaspoon of turmeric powder together. Add this to the snakegourd and mix.

3. Add the thick coconut milk and cook uncovered for 10–15 minutes. The result will be very tender snakegourd and a rich, vivid yellow curry.

Meats

Although Sri Lanka is predominantly a Buddhist nation, we love our meat. Every ethnic group is famous for one meat dish. The Burghers are well known for their black pork curry. The Sinhalese, for their red chicken curry. For the Moors, it is their tender, water-based beef curry. And for the Tamils, their delicious mutton pooriyal. Every group tends to clear steer of eating one kind of meat (like beef for the Sinhalese and Tamils, and pork for the Moors). Moor 'hotels' (roadside cafes) are the best for the meat-curious, many of which serve more unique dishes like brain curry, tripe (babath), gizzard, kidney and liver curries. This is an experience I would highly recommend when in Sri Lanka.

A lot of the meat dishes in this section are prepared with traditional ingredients, but I have refined the technique to produce a much more delicious result. For instance, some recipes call for finishing in the oven, which is not the traditional Sri Lankan way but is meant to mimic open hearth cooking, where they place hot coals and firewood on the top and bottom of the dish. A lot of the big curries call for slow cooking but trust me, if you follow through, you will be rewarded!

mutton pooriyal

Serves **2-4** | Time **1 hour 40 minutes** | Ethnic Roots **Ceylon Tamil/Indian Tamil**

INGREDIENTS

For the first step:

4 garlic cloves, minced

1 red onion, roughly chopped

1½ tbsps tomato paste

1 tsp pepper

1 litre of chicken or beef stock

500g boneless mutton

1 tbsp fennel seeds

1 tbsp cumin seeds

1 tbsp coriander powder

1 tsp cinnamon powder

4 whole cloves

For the temper:

2 tbsps ghee or oil

1 red onion, thinly sliced in half moons

8 curry leaves

3 green chillies, chopped

4 garlic cloves, minced

2 tbsps Jaffna curry powder

1½ tsps sugar

2 tsps salt

½ tsp black pepper

1 tbsp vinegar

METHOD

1. Place all the ingredients for the first step into the pressure cooker, close it and place over a medium heat. Let it cook for 30–40 minutes (or 5 whistles). Check the mutton, it should be very tender. If not, then run your pressure cooker for another 10 minutes. If you don't have a pressure cooker, then cook the meat over a low to medium flame in a stockpot covered for 1–1.5 hours.

2. In a large frying pan, heat the ghee over a medium high heat. Add in the onion, curry leaves, green chillies and fry for 3 minutes until the onion caramelizes.

3. Add the minced garlic and fry for another 2 minutes before tipping in the contents of the pressure cooker (mutton, spices and broth). Stir occasionally for 5 minutes or until the broth has reduced by half. Add in the Jaffna curry powder, the sugar, the salt and black pepper. Mix well and cook for a further 5 minutes.

4. By now there should be very little broth left. Add in the vinegar and fry until all the broth has evaporated and you are left with a very dark, dry, tempered curry. Serve with pittu, hoppers or rice!

jaggery beef curry

Serves **4** | Time **2 hours 45 minutes** | Ethnic Roots **Sinhalese/Malay**

INGREDIENTS

3 tbsps ghee

800g beef rib, beef cheek or beef shin, cut into equal chunks (a cut with a good level of animal fat running through it for slow cooking)

1 red onion (150g), chopped

15 curry leaves

5 large garlic cloves, chopped

40g ginger, minced

10 whole cloves

5 cardamoms, lightly pounded

1 tsp cumin seeds, pounded

1 cinnamon quill

240ml coconut water

340g bone marrow

4 tbsps roasted curry powder

2 tsps salt

2 tbsps roasted chilli powder

1 1/2 tbsps turmeric powder

400ml thin coconut milk

2 tbsps tamarind paste

400ml thick coconut milk

30g jaggery (can substitute with very dark, treacle-like sugar or palm sugar)

My favourite version of this special dish belongs to my friend Venya's family. They cook it over a woodfire for several hours in a clay pot, with ground coriander and mint leaves. However, I have come up with a simple yet effective recipe that yields a great result. If you do have time, you can brine the beef in a salt solution for 1–2 hours before you cook it for a very tender result!

METHOD

1. In a deep-bottomed stock pot, heat 2 tablespoons of ghee. Brown the meat in batches making sure that there is good caramelization on it. The meat will release its fat, adding flavour to the temper. Set the meat aside to rest whilst prepping the other ingredients.

2. To the same stock pot, add in 1 tablespoon of ghee. When hot, add the onions and cook till they soften. Next, add the curry leaves, garlic, ginger and all the whole spices and fry for 30 seconds. Pour in the coconut water and cook for 3 minutes. Add in the meat, the bone marrow and mix in the curry powder, 1 teaspoon salt, roasted chilli and turmeric powder. Mix well. Add in the thin coconut milk, tamarind paste and cook for 1 hour on a medium-low flame.

3. Pour in the thick coconut milk and add 1 teaspoon salt. Cook it for a further 1.5 hours or until the meat is tender. This last step can also be done in the oven. If you do decide to finish the curry in the oven, make sure that the meat is covered with a lid, and stir it occasionally to ensure no sticking at the bottom of the pot.

4. Once the curry has cooked through, take it off the heat and add in the jaggery. Stir to make sure the jaggery is fully incorporated into the gravy. Serve with piping hot fluffy basmati rice!

lamb curd curry

Serves **4** | Time **2 hours 10 minutes** | Ethnic Roots **Ceylon Tamil/Ceylon Moor**

INGREDIENTS

620g lamb shoulder, boneless, cut into
equal-sized pieces

3 tbsps unroasted curry powder

2 tbsps roasted chilli powder

1 tbsp cumin seeds

1 tsp turmeric powder

1 tsp mustard seeds

1 tsp nutmeg powder (or fresh grated nutmeg)

240g buffalo curd or greek yoghurt

2 tbsps ghee/ sunflower oil

1 red onion, diced

5 curry leaves

10 cardamom pods, pounded

3 garlic cloves, minced

30g ginger, minced

2 fresh green chillies, minced

150g tomatoes, diced

2 tsps tomato paste

600ml water

10 stalks of coriander, stalks and leaves chopped

METHOD

1. In a large bowl, mix the lamb pieces, curry powder, chilli powder, cumin seeds, turmeric powder, mustard seeds, nutmeg and yoghurt together and marinate for at least 1 hour.

2. In a large stock pot, heat the ghee or oil over a medium heat. Add in the onion, curry leaves and pounded cardamoms. Fry for a few minutes, till the onion turns golden. Immediately add in the garlic, ginger and green chilli. Cook for another 2-3 minutes. Mix in the tomato pieces, the tomato paste and cook for another 3–4 minutes.

3. Add in the marinated lamb and mix well. Cook for 5–8 minutes and add in 400ml of water. Cook covered for 40 minutes on medium-low heat. Check the curry, if it looks a little dry add 100ml of water. Put in the chopped coriander leaves and mix well. Transfer the lamb into a preheated oven (180°C) for 60 minutes or cook until meat is tender over a low flame. Once the meat is tender and the curry runs thick, remove from the oven or stove, add in another 50–100ml of water to loosen the curry, mix well and garnish with coriander leaves. Serve with rice or hot rotis!

Usually in Sri Lanka, people do not have the privilege of eating lamb, and in supermarkets you will see two types of mutton—local (goat) and imported (sheep). So, back in Lanka they would usually make this curry with goat, but lamb also makes for a delicious and tender result. So, use what you can get—it turns out great.

black pork curry

Serves **4-6** | Time **3 hours 12 minutes** | Ethnic Roots **Burgher**

INGREDIENTS

To marinate the pork:

1kg trimmed pork belly (save the fat and skin), cut into equal-sized pieces

3 tbsps roasted curry powder

1 tbsp roasted chilli powder

2 tsps turmeric powder

1 tsp cardamom powder (or 6 cardamom pods)

1 tsp cinnamon powder

1 tbsp white vinegar

1 tsp cumin powder

1 tsp coriander powder

1 tbsp ground black pepper

The thickener:

2 tbsps desiccated coconut

1 tbsp basmati rice

For the curry:

20g goraka

150ml water

3 tbsps virgin coconut oil

5 shallots, diced

20 curry leaves

½ tbsp fenugreek

6 cloves

2 heads of lemongrass, bashed and left whole

3 fresh green chillies, minced

5 large garlic cloves, minced

30g of ginger, minced

1200 ml water

½ tbsp tamarind paste/concentrate

1 tsp sea salt

Juice of ½ lime

METHOD

1. In a bowl, mix all the ingredients for the marinade along with the pork and set aside. Marinate for at least 30 minutes.

2. In a small frying pan, roast the desiccated coconut and the basmati rice for 3–4 minutes or until the mixture starts to lightly brown. Immediately take off the heat and grind to a powder.

3. In a small pan over a medium heat, boil the goraka with 150ml of water until all the water is evaporated and the goraka is softened. Grind into a paste and set aside.

4. Heat 1 tbsp of coconut oil in a deep stockpot or pan, over medium heat. Add in the trimmed fat and skin and render the fat into the oil. Remove the cooked fat and skin and set aside.

5. Add the additional 2 tablespoons coconut oil to the pork flavoured oil. Next, add in the shallots, curry leaves, fenugreek, cloves and lemongrass. Fry for 3–4 minutes and then add the fresh chilli, garlic and ginger. Sauté until the shallots start to caramelize. To this add the pork and mix well. If you find the pan is starting to catch at the bottom, add some water (60ml or ¼ cup of water) to the pork.

6. After 4–5 minutes of browning the pork, add the rice-coconut powder, all the water and mix well. Cook for 10 minutes. Then add in the tamarind concentrate and the goraka paste. Mix well and cook for an hour over medium-low heat.

7. Add the sea salt, transfer the pot to the oven and cook at 180°C for 1.5 hours. Alternatively, cook on a low flame, the pork should be tender with thick gravy. If a lot of liquid remains in the curry, place it over a high heat and reduce for another 10 minutes. Immediately add in the lime juice and mix well. Let it sit for 10 minutes before serving.

One of the most famous dishes that belongs to the Burgher community, the black pork curry is a star amongst curries. Served the world over either in trendy Lankan restaurants or in every Burgher home, Sri Lankans love this curry! Pair with yellow rice and pol sambol.

buhari-inspired roast chicken

Serves **4** | Prep **3 hours/overnight** | Time **35 minutes** | Ethnic Roots **Ceylon Moor**

INGREDIENTS

Prepare the whole chicken:

1.5 kilo free range chicken, butchered into the following pieces (bone in, skin on)

  4 pieces of chicken breast

  2 chicken thighs

  2 drumsticks

  2 wings

Prepare the marinade for the chicken:

3 tsps Kashmiri red chilli powder

2 tsps salt

1 tsp cumin powder

1 tsp coriander powder

Juice of 1 lime

For the frying:

60g (¼ cup) of ghee

2 tbsps of ghee

20 curry leaves

6 inches pandan leaf, torn

3 small shallots, ground into paste

30g garlic, ground into paste

30g ginger, ground into paste

1 tsp cumin powder

1 tsp coriander powder

1 tsp Kashmiri red chilli powder

½ tsp turmeric powder

1 tsp salt

Juice of 2 limes

METHOD

1. Fill a large Ziploc bag, with all the marinade ingredients except the lime juice and give it a good shake so that the spices are well combined. Put the chicken pieces into the ziplock bag and seal it. Shake the bag vigorously ensuring that the chicken pieces are well-coated in the dry rub. Reopen the bag, add the lime juice and massage unto the chicken pieces. Seal the bag, place in the fridge and marinate overnight or for at least 3 hours.

2. Melt the ¼ cup of ghee in a frying pan; make sure that the pan has enough oil to cook all the chicken pieces. Do not shake the rub off the chicken as it adds to the flavour and helps create the crispy bits on it. Working in batches, fry the dark and the white meat separately. Cook the chicken on all sides, frying each side for a minimum of five minutes, till the chicken turns a dark golden colour and is cooked through. Set the pieces aside to cool.

3. Melt 2 tablespoons of ghee in a wok on a medium-high heat. Once the ghee is hot, add in the curry leaves and pandan leaves and fry for 1–2 minutes. Add in the ground shallots, ginger and garlic paste and stir continuously for 2 minutes.

4. Tip in all the ground spices to the temper and fry for 1 minute, then quickly add in the chicken pieces. Fry for 5 minutes, coating the pieces in the masala paste. Add in the salt, mix well and drizzle the chicken with the lime juice. Cook further for a few minutes until the chicken is very fragrant. Serve with lime wedges and roti.

Serving Muslim cuisine, Hotel De Buhari is an institution in Maradana, Colombo. And they make an incredible masala roast chicken. In Sri Lanka, when people refer to 'roast', it usually means that the chicken is boiled, then deep fried and served with a masala gravy. This tends to result in very dry chicken; however the Buhari chicken has a masala that is unrivalled. This recipe is inspired by this chicken but is juicier with a few twists! The trick to this recipe is the use of Kashmiri red chilli powder—it is critical to getting the flavour right. For best results use a free range or organic chicken with the skin on (that's where all the flavour is!).

egg curry

Serves **2–4** | Time **30 minutes** | Ethnic Roots **Sinhalese/Multi-ethnic**

INGREDIENTS

4 eggs, peeled, boiled and halved

1 tbsp sunflower/coconut oil

1 large shallot (25g), chopped

2 large garlic cloves, chopped

3 inches fresh lemongrass, cut into 3 pieces, pounded

2 fresh green chillies, chopped

6 curry leaves

1 tsp turmeric powder

½ large tomato, chopped

180ml water

180ml coconut milk

1 tsp salt

Simple to execute and very satisfying, this is every Sri Lankan's go-to breakfast curry. It can be paired with a number of breads or rice dishes. The eggs can be boiled the way you like them—I like them a little gooey in the middle. This gravy or 'hodi' in this recipe is also known as a kiri hodi (a milk gravy); one which is usually served for more simple meals like stringhoppers and pol sambol, or poured over white rice with some vegetarian curries.

METHOD

1. In a deep saucepan, bring water to the boil and carefully lower every egg into the boiling water. Reduce the heat to a simmer and cook for 6 minutes. Remove from the pan and immediately dunk in cold water to stop the cooking. You can store the boiled eggs in their shells in the fridge until you are ready to cook the curry (can be done 3 days ahead).

2. In a small pan, heat 1 tablespoon of sunflower/coconut oil. When the oil is warm, add in the shallot. Fry for two minutes, then add in the garlic, lemongrass, green chillies and curry leaves.

3. Add the turmeric powder and chopped tomato, and mix well.

4. Immediately pour in the water and cook the mixture for 5 minutes before adding the coconut milk. Add 1 teaspoon of salt. Cook for 10 minutes or until the gravy acquires a soup like consistency.

5. Deshell and halve your eggs or keep them whole; depends on how you like to present your food. Add in the eggs and make sure that they are well covered in the sauce. Serve with string hoppers and pol sambol.

red chicken curry

Serves **4** | Time **1 hour** | Ethnic Roots **Sinhalese**

INGREDIENTS

Marinade for the chicken:

500g bone-in chicken thighs (or whole chicken
pieces cut up), skin on

2 tsps red chilli powder

1 tsp unroasted curry powder

½ tsp turmeric powder

½ tsp salt

For the curry:

20g tamarind or 1½ tsps tamarind paste

360ml thin coconut milk (if tinned, 240ml
coconut milk diluted with 120ml water)

2 tbsps coconut oil

1 small red onion, diced

10 curry leaves

½ stem lemongrass, lightly pounded with the
back of a knife

5 cm piece of a pandan leaf

1 tsp mustard seeds

½ cinnamon quill

1 tsp fenugreek seeds

20g garlic and 20g fresh ginger, ground to make
a paste

3 cloves

2 cardamoms, pounded

1 fresh green chilli, diced

1½ tsps red chilli powder

120ml thick coconut milk

*I keep the skin on the chicken (a cardinal
sin in Sri Lanka!) and slow-cook this one. If
you can, go the extra mile, try and butcher a
whole chicken yourself and use all the different
pieces to add depth to the curry including the
backbone. It produces the most delicious result.*

METHOD

1. In a bowl, add the chicken, red chilli powder, curry powder, turmeric powder and salt. Massage the spices into the chicken and marinate for 10 minutes.

2. Mix the tamarind pieces in the thin coconut milk. Strain and set aside. If using tamarind paste, simply mix it into the coconut milk, ensuring all of it is dissolved.

3. In a deep saucepan with a lid or a Dutch oven, heat the coconut oil over a medium fire. Add the red onion, curry leaves, lemongrass, pandan leaf, mustard seeds, cinnamon quill and fenugreek seeds. Fry for 2 minutes before adding garlic-ginger paste, cloves, cardamoms and fresh green chilli. Cook for a further 2–3 minutes, before adding the chicken.

4. Sauté the chicken pieces until it turns golden brown. Pour in the thin coconut milk and cook covered for 20 minutes.

5. In a small pan, roast the additional 1½ teaspoons of red chilli powder for 1 minute or until it turns a little darker. Quickly add the roasted chilli powder into the chicken curry and mix well. This brings the 'red' colour to the chicken curry. Cook covered for 5 minutes.

6. Next, add in the thick coconut milk and mix well. Cook covered for a further 15 minutes on a low heat until a beautiful red gravy has formed and the chicken is cooked through.

Tip: If you want a redder curry, stir in 1 teaspoon of tomato paste into the curry when you mix in the thick coconut milk.

black chicken curry

INGREDIENTS

For the black curry powder:

1 tbsp white rice

2 tsps coriander seeds

1 tsp fennel seeds

1 tsp cumin seeds

1 tsp whole peppercorns

4 cloves

4 cardamoms

6 dried red chillies

2 tbsps grated coconut

8 curry leaves

For the rest of the curry:

500g chicken thighs and chicken drumsticks (4 pieces)

2 tsps of salt

¼ tsp turmeric paste or powder

3 garlic cloves (10–15g)

1 inch ginger (20 g)

120ml thick coconut milk

2 tsps tamarind paste

2 tbsps coconut oil

½ red onion (50g), chopped

3-inch piece of pandan leaf, torn into strips

½ tsp fenugreek seeds

½ tsp mustard seeds

1 stick lemongrass, chopped into 3 pieces

1 fresh green chilli, chopped

1 piece cinnamon (5g)

6 curry leaves

¼ tsp red chilli powder

240ml thin coconut milk

240ml water

METHOD

1. In a frying pan over a high heat, roast the rice, coriander seeds, fennel seeds, cumin seeds, peppercorns, cloves and cardamoms, stirring constantly for 2 minutes. Add in the dried red chillies and roast for a further 4 minutes. The spices are done when the rice is browned, and the spices are fragrant. Set aside. In the same frying pan, roast the grated coconut and curry leaves for 3½ –4 minutes over a medium heat. Let it cool for a few minutes, before grinding it into a fine black curry powder.

2. In a bowl, rub the chicken with 1 teaspoon of salt and ¼ teaspoon of turmeric powder.

3. In a pestle and mortar or a spice grinder, pound the garlic and ginger into a rough paste.

4. Mix 120ml thick coconut milk with the tamarind paste in a bowl. Set aside.

5. In a deep saucepan, heat the coconut oil over a medium fire and fry the onion, pandan, fenugreek seeds, mustard seeds, lemongrass, green chilli, cinnamon and curry leaves. Fry for 3 minutes, add the ginger-garlic paste and cook for another 2 minutes. Next, add in the chicken pieces, ¼ teaspoon of red chilli powder and brown for 4 minutes.

6. Mix in half the black curry powder. Fry the chicken and black curry powder for a further 3 minutes before adding 240ml of coconut milk and water to the pan. Stir well, and cook covered for 5 minutes.

7. Stir in the tamarind-spiked thick coconut milk into the curry. Cover the pan and continue to cook it for a further 10 minutes.

8. Add in the rest of the black curry powder and mix well. Cook uncovered for another 10 minutes and the curry is ready.

Deep, dark and roasted, black curry is an instant classic in Sri Lanka. However, each meat requires a different method to achieve its dark, rich flavour. This recipe requires you to grind your own spices, and if you do make the effort, the results are quite exceptional. But, if you do not have the time, you can substitute it with a roasted curry powder, but you need the roasted ground rice and roasted ground coconut. Again, for the best results, I would use a whole chicken, butchered, with the skin on.

sri lankan fried chicken (SLFC)

Serves **4** | Prep **5 hours/overnight** | Time **30 minutes** | Ethnic Roots **Multi-ethnic**

INGREDIENTS

Marinate overnight:

250ml milk

2 tbsps apple cider vinegar

2 tsps chilli powder

1 tsp turmeric paste/powder

1½ tsps salt

12 wings, cut into drumlets, wingettes and tips off

For the dredge:

200g rice flour

100g corn flour

2 tbsps unroasted curry powder

1 tbsp chilli powder

2 tsps salt

250ml neutral oil

Growing up in Sri Lanka in the early nineties, the closest thing one could get that would be considered 'western' food was crumb-fried chicken or 'chicken in a basket'. Keeping allergies in mind, I have come up with a gluten-free version of fried chicken. Eat with lots of hot sauce and French fries!

METHOD

1. Take a large Ziploc bag and pour in the milk, apple cider vinegar, chilli powder, turmeric powder and salt. Seal the bag and shake well until all the ingredients are well combined. Add in the prepared wingettes and drumlets, seal, then shake ensuring that the wings are submerged in the marinade. Alternatively, use a large mixing bowl to combine all the ingredients and cover with clingfilm. Leave overnight or for at least 5 hours.

2. In a separate mixing bowl, combine the rice flour, corn flour, curry powder, chilli powder and salt. Make sure the spices are well-distributed through the flour.

3. Heat a medium pan over a medium-high flame and pour in 250ml of oil. Take the marinated wings and dredge it in the seasoned flour. Make sure that they are coated well. Working in batches, carefully lower 4–5 wing pieces into the hot oil and fry until light golden (about 4–5 minutes). Drain the wings over some kitchen towel and set aside for the second fry. Once all the pieces have been fried once, bring the oil to temperature and add the wings in batches again and fry for another 5–6 minutes until they are golden-brown. Drain the excess oil on a kitchen towel.

beef smore

Serves **4-6** | Time **2 hours 45 minutes** | Ethnic Roots **Burgher**

INGREDIENTS

1kg beef brisket (or a roasting cut)

2 tsps salt

3 tbsps ghee

450g red onions, diced

10–15 curry leaves

30g lemongrass (2 large stalks), bashed but left whole

1 cinnamon quill (5g), broken in two

10 cloves

50g garlic cloves, minced

40g ginger, sliced

6 cardamoms, bashed

4 tbsps unroasted curry powder

1 tsp turmeric powder

1 tbsp black peppercorns

3 tbsps vinegar

1 tsp sugar

4 small green chillies, halved

1 litre beef stock

400ml thick coconut milk

Another Burgher classic, the beef smore is a highly sought-after dish. My mother loves to order it from the Dutch Burgher Union in Colombo. There are different interpretations of this dish—some serve this dish cut into pieces reminiscent of most Lankan beef curries, whereas others stay true to the dish's Eurasian roots and serve it as a pot roast; sliced and then doused in the curry sauce. This is the style of this recipe—and unlike a pot roast, this is meant to be eaten with rice!

METHOD

1. Sprinkle 1 teaspoon of salt over the beef cut, making sure to cover all sides. In a large Dutch oven or an ovenproof saucepan, heat the 2 tablespoons of ghee over a medium-high heat. Next, brown the brisket on all sides. The meat should have formed a crust on some parts of the piece. This Maillard reaction will bring flavour to the beef and the dish as it cooks. Set aside.

2. In the pot, melt 1 tablespoon of ghee and add in the red onions. Sweat the onions, until they start to caramelize, about 4–5 minutes. If the pan is drying out add 1 tablespoon of ghee. Next add in the curry leaves, the lemongrass, cinnamon quills, the cloves, garlic, ginger and the cardamoms and fry for another 3–4 minutes.

3. Add the brisket back into the pot, add in the unroasted curry powder, turmeric and pepper. Fry for 2 minutes, make sure to coat the meat well in the spices. Add a little water if the spices start to stick or burn. Mix in the vinegar, the sugar, green chillies and the stock. Bring it to the boil and turn down the heat to low. At this stage, it would be best to transfer this to the oven, and cook at 180°C or continue to cook over the stove for at least an hour. Stir halfway to make sure it is well combined.

4. After an hour, add the thick coconut milk, the remaining salt and cook for 1–1.5 hours depending on the quality of your cut. The meat should be tender and easy to slice. Remove any whole spices and the lemongrass once cooked. Rest the beef for at least 10 minutes before serving.

omelette curry

Serves **2–4** | Time **40 minutes** | Ethnic Roots **Sinhalese/Multi-ethnic**

INGREDIENTS

For the omelette:

30g garlic (4–5 large cloves), chopped

30g peeled ginger, chopped

1 tsp cumin seeds

1 tsp salt

½ tsp turmeric paste

4 large eggs

70g red onion, diced

2 green chillies, minced

1 ½ tsps lime juice

1–2 tbsps neutral oil

For the hodi:

2 tbsps neutral oil

120g red onion

3-inch piece pandan leaf

8 to 10 curry leaves

1 tbsp tomato paste

2 tsps unroasted curry powder

1 tsp chilli powder

1 tsp mustard seeds

1 tsp turmeric paste/powder

1 green chilli, minced

220ml water

200ml thick coconut milk

1 tsp salt

Juice of ½ lime

METHOD

1. In a spice grinder or food processor, blend the garlic and ginger with 2 tablespoons of water until you have a fine paste. Set aside half the paste for the hodi and then add the cumin seeds, salt and turmeric paste to the spice grinder and blend until you have a fine paste.

2. In a mixing bowl, whisk the eggs, the turmeric-cumin-garlic-ginger paste, the red onion, minced chillies and lime juice together until well incorporated. Heat a large frying pan and bring the oil to temperature. Pour in the contents of the egg mixture and cook over a medium heat, till it turns a light golden colour. After two minutes, carefully flip the omelette on the other side to ensure even cooking. Cook for another minute and transfer to a plate to rest. At this time, with a sharp knife cut it into at least 10–12 equal strips.

3. In the same frying pan, add another 2 tablespoons of oil and heat over a medium heat. Add in the onions, pandan leaf and the curry leaves, and shallow-fry for 2–3 minutes, before adding in the tomato paste and cooking till it caramelizes. Fry for a further 2 minutes before adding the unroasted curry powder, chilli powder, turmeric, mustard seeds and minced green chilli. Mix it well and fry for another 2 minutes. If it's starting to catch, add 60ml–120ml of water depending on the heat level and the size of frying pan. Once the raw smell of the spices is gone (about 2 minutes), add in 150ml of the coconut milk and cook for a minute before adding in 100ml of water. Cook on a low heat for 4 minutes. Add in the remaining 50ml of coconut milk and salt, and cook for another 2 minutes.

4. Turn the heat to low and add in the omelette strips, carefully fold them into the gravy ensuring that the pieces stay intact. Cook for 2 minutes and take off the heat. Squeeze the lime over the curry and let it sit for a few minutes before stirring and serving.

Desserts

As a food culture, Sri Lankans were not big on desserts. Previously, one could argue that desserts were only served for special occasions—dishes like sweetmeats and wattalapan were made for festivals, weddings and celebrations. However, in the last 150 years or so, it is very evident that Sri Lankans love sugar. This demonstrated in our 'tea culture', which is either made with condensed milk or with four teaspoons of sugar!

Before fancy American-style desserts flooded our restaurants and homes, one of the staple party desserts was a fruit cocktail with a big dollop of vanilla ice cream! Who could forget the humble but delicious curd and treacle—no Sri Lankan dessert table is complete unless there is a pot of buffalo curd. Other famed desserts were a butter cake and a date cake; and at teatime, if cake was unavailable, Sri Lankans would turn to a good biscuit. Lankans are addicted to biscuits, eating a whopping 86,400,000 kilos a year!

This section has a selection of traditional and modern recipes; make sure you are ready to indulge that sweet tooth though, because we Lankans love our 'tin kiri' (tin or condensed milk)!

Greedy Andare

Andare is a fictional court jester, whose stories are often told to Sri Lankan children. An excellent storyteller, my late Seeya (Sinhalese for grandfather) Reggie would recount the tales of Andare to my cousins and me, at his kitchen table. He would often tell us the story of 'Greedy Andare' before we had any desserts at his house—an apt tale to remember every time you have a Sri Lankan sweet treat!

ANDARE AND THE KIRI PANI

The King was tired of being consistently outdone by his court jester, Andare—it was humiliating that a king of his great stature could not outwit a 'lowly court jester'. So, unknown to Andare, the King plotted a new scheme that would surely fix his friendly nemesis! A royal banquet was planned and a messenger was sent to Andare's home to invite him. The royal chefs were instructed by the King to prepare all of Andare's favourite dishes to serve at the gala event.

The day of the banquet arrived. Andare could not believe the spread on offer: the banquet table was groaning under the weight of countless delectable dishes, with many of his favourite curries making their appearance too! Filled with gluttony, Andare enthusiastically proceeded to eat. He helped himself to one large serving after another of rice and curry until he lay back on his dining chair, rubbed his big rice belly, and declared he could not eat another morsel. The King, watching with devilish glee as greed overcame the court jester, asked Andare to have one more helping of food. Andare flatly refused, proclaiming if he ate another bite, he would surely collapse. The King urged Andare once more, and he refused yet again.

Satisfied at Andare's repeated refusals to eat, the King asked the servers to clear the table, and bring in the dessert course. Immediately, Andare's mood changed; the thought of a sweet treat piqued his interest. The chefs placed bowls of buffalo curd with thick lashings of kithul pani (local treacle) in front of the guests. This was Andare's favourite dish; he instantly hopped over the table to help himself to the kiri pani and started to greedily gorge on it. The King took this chance! He accused Andare of lying to him; how could Andare eat more when only a few moments earlier he refused rice and curry citing that another morsel would ensure his collapse! The King gave Andare an ultimatum: explain his sudden ability to eat more or suffer a terrible punishment.

But Andare was a clever man. He begged the King for his permission to demonstrate his answer. The King, sure that he had finally trumped the jester, allowed Andare to proceed. Andare asked the royal guards to fill a room with as many subjects loyal to the King as possible and to inform him when not one more person could fit into the room. After a few hours, the guards informed Andare that they had completed the task. Andare took the King to the room brimming to the door with his subjects and yelled, 'Make way for the King! The King is coming.' There were sounds of shuffling feet, and then a small but distinct path formed for the King to enter the room. 'This is how I could make room for the kiri pani, Your Highness,' declared Andare; once again besting the King.

I hope that after eating a sizeable portion of rice and curry, you too can be like Andare and make room for a delicious sweet treat from this section of the book.

salted lankan caramelized bananas

Serves **2-3** | Time **15 minutes** | Ethnic Roots **Sinhalese**

INGREDIENTS

10g butter

4 tbsps demerara sugar/ brown sugar

4 tbsps water

4 very ripe ambul bananas (sour banana), sliced lengthwise in half

½ tsp sea-salt flakes

This is a recipe I use when I need to whip up a quick snack with tea. This is even better when served with a scoop of vanilla ice cream or a dollop of whipped cream or some vanilla custard!

METHOD

1. In a large frying pan, add the butter, brown sugar and water. Over a medium heat, allow the ingredients to melt and combine. Swirl the pan (without stirring it) every 20 seconds to make sure that the butter, sugar and water are well combined. A caramel should start to form within 4 minutes.

2. As the caramel starts to form and bubble vigorously, quickly add in the sliced bananas ensuring that they are covered in the sauce but they stay whole. Immediately lower the heat so that the caramel does not burn.

3. After 4 minutes, the sauce should have penetrated the bananas. At this point, crush and sprinkle the sea salt over the bananas and give them a quick mix.

4. Serve the bananas while warm.

lime coconut cake

Serves **8-12** | Time **1 hour 40 minutes** | Ethnic Roots **British heritage**

INGREDIENTS

For the cake batter:

250g butter (room temperature)

250g white caster sugar

4 eggs (room temperature)

1 tsp vanilla extract

100ml coconut milk

The zest of 3 limes, reserve the juice for the buttercream

250g plain flour

1 tsp baking soda

½ tsp baking powder

¼ tsp salt

30g of desiccated coconut

For the buttercream:

200g butter, at room temperature

200g icing sugar

Juice of 3 limes

3 tsps of high-quality gin

Growing up, if it was an occasion with my extended family, a butter cake was always served along with strong milk tea. My mum would always put a lime icing on top of the cake for an added twist on this teatime staple. Taking that as the inspiration, I have developed this lime coconut cake which if you take my mum's word for it is 'just divine'.

METHOD

1. Preheat the oven to 180°C. Line two 2x8-inch diameter non-stick cake trays with parchment paper.

2. In a freestanding mixer, or with an electric beater, work the butter and sugar until thick and creamy. To prevent the butter from splitting and ruining the cake, take care to not overbeat the batter.

3. Beat the eggs into the butter-and-sugar mixture on medium, one at a time, making sure that each is fully incorporated before adding in another. Add in the vanilla. This should be a very thick batter at this stage.

4. Beat in the coconut milk and lime zest. Mix well. At this stage the batter should be thick and fluffy.

5. Sift together the flour, baking soda, baking powder and salt. Fold it into the batter making sure to envelop in as much air as possible with every fold. Once all the flour is incorporated, the batter should be fluffy and light.

6. Divide the batter in half, and split it between the two cake tins. Bake the cakes in the oven for 50 minutes, this may vary depending on the heat of your oven. The cakes should be golden in colour. To check if the cake is cooked through, prick it with a skewer and if it comes out clean, it's done. Once done, allow them to cool completely. Next, with an electric mixer, cream the butter and the icing sugar together and mix well until it starts to resemble heavy whipping cream. At this stage, add the lime juice and the gin and beat until well mixed. The buttercream should be light and fluffy.

7. Place one cake on a large plate or tray and layer buttercream on top of the cake (not the sides), then sandwich the second cake on top and cover the top of that layer with the rest of the buttercream. Decorate with coconut flakes.

no-churn coconut, rum and banana ice cream

Makes **one loaf tin of ice cream** | Time **6 hours**

INGREDIENTS

400 ml whipping cream

260ml condensed milk

3 tbsp good quality dark rum

200g banana (frozen or room temp), chopped

1 tsp vanilla extract

120 ml coconut milk

METHOD

1. In a cold large bowl, using an electric beater or a hand whisk, whip the cream until soft peaks are formed.

2. In a separate bowl, whisk the condensed milk with the rum until well incorporated.

3. In a food processor or a grinder, add the bananas, vanilla extract and coconut milk and puree until smooth.

4. Take two large serving spoons of the whipped cream and whisk into the condensed milk-rum mixture to loosen the mix. Then fold it into the whipped cream and combine well. Finally whisk in the banana-coconut mixture, beating as much air as possible into the ice-cream mixture.

5. Pour the mixture into a standardized Pyrex bread tin loaf, cover with clingfilm and put in the freezer for 6 hours. Every 2 hours, give the ice cream a good mix, scraping the sides of the tin. If you aren't too bothered, you can simply freeze it without hand-mixing it.

6. After 6 hours, the ice cream will be ready to eat! Serve with fresh fruit or with a salted jaggery sauce (see p. 229).

salted jaggery caramel sauce

Makes **approximately 300ml** | Time **20 minutes**

INGREDIENTS

100g jaggery, broken into pieces

50g light muscovado sugar or brown sugar

50g butter, cold and cut into cubes

250ml heavy whipping cream/ double cream

¾ tsp sea salt flakes

METHOD

1. Place a frying pan over a high heat and add in the jaggery. Allow it to melt for 2 minutes and then turn the flame down to a medium.

2. Once half the jaggery is melted, immediately add in the sugar and whisk them together. It is important that they start to combine.

3. After a few minutes of whisking the sugar and jaggery (approximately 3 minutes), add in the cubed cold butter and allow it to melt for a minute before starting to whisk again.

4. Once the butter and jaggery are melted and mixed, immediately add in the whipping cream and whisk until well incorporated. Next, whisk in the sea salt flakes.

5. Once the salt is dissolved, allow it to cool a little before pouring the ingredients into an empty jar. Once the sauce has cooled completely, store it in the refrigerator. It lasts up to 1 month. Pour over ice cream and fruit for a yummy treat!

tin kiri
crème caramel

Serves **4-6** | Time **1 hour** | Ethnic Roots **European heritage**

INGREDIENTS

For the caramel:
110g white granulated sugar
3 tbsps water

For the custard:
450g condensed milk
3 eggs and 1 egg yolk
450ml full-fat milk
2 tsps vanilla extract

METHOD

1. Preheat the oven to 180°C. Have a medium-sized round ovenproof dish ready (approximately 8-inch diameter) before starting to cook. It is important that the base of the dish is much smaller in circumference than the top of the dish.

2. Put the sugar and the water for the caramel into a small pan and lightly mix, so that they are combined before cooking.

3. Place the pan on a high heat for 4 minutes until a brown caramel forms. Every 45 seconds swirl (not stir) the pan to ensure even cooking. Time this step, as that will ensure a perfect caramel. Once the caramel has developed a dark golden-brown colour (it takes approximately 2 minutes to turn dark brown from golden), immediately remove from the heat and pour it into the base of the dish. Work fast, and quickly swirl the caramel to fully cover the base of the dish, along with a bit of the sides as well. Set aside to cool.

4. In a mixing bowl, whisk the condensed milk, eggs, milk and vanilla extract till a custard-like batter is formed.

5. Pour the custard batter into the caramel-laced dish, take care to not fill it to the top. Cover the dish with a lid or with aluminium foil. Place a shallow ovenproof pan filled with water into the oven to help create a steam oven. Place the crème caramel dish into the oven and cook for 35–40 minutes or until the custard has set. Remove from the oven and allow it to cool.

6. Once the custard has cooled, run a small sharp knife around the circumference of the dish to help separate the pudding from the sides of the dish. Place a large plate on top of the dish and turn out the pudding onto the plate. The caramel should have cooked the bottom of the pudding so it is much darker in colour to the rest of the pudding. Spoon the leftover caramel syrup from the bowl over the rest of the pudding and serve.

ribbon birthday cake

INGREDIENTS

Dry ingredients:

1 tsps baking soda

2 tsps baking powder

360g cake flour

1 tsp salt

Wet ingredients:

240ml milk or single cream

1 tbsp white vinegar

350g white caster sugar or granulated sugar

100g brown sugar

150g butter, cubed and softened

4 eggs

2 ½ tsps vanilla extract

100ml sunflower or neutral oil

1 tsp pink colouring, depends on your brand

1 tsp green colouring, depends on your brand

150g rainbow sprinkles

For the icing:

300g butter (room temperature)

300g icing sugar

150g cream cheese

1 tsp vanilla extract

Sri Lankans love a good cake and this one is often served at birthday parties. All ribbon cakes are two layers—one green, one pink; a celebration for sure. However, my biggest issue with this cake is that it is often dry, so I have added in a buttermilk substitute to make sure the cake is moist and light. For your next party, give it a go!

METHOD

1. Preheat the oven to 180°C. Prepare three 9-inch round cake pans with parchment paper at the bottom of each tin, and set aside.

2. Sift all the dry ingredients and set aside.

3. In a bowl, or a measuring jug, mix together the milk and the white vinegar and set aside for 10 minutes to sour the mixture and create a buttermilk.

4. Beat the white sugar, brown sugar and butter together with an electric beater until well creamed. Add one egg, beat until well incorporated and then add the next egg. Repeat for all the eggs. A thick, ribbony batter should be formed. Add in the vanilla extract and mix well.

5. Whisk your buttermilk and oil together in a jug. Add 1/3 of this mixture and 1/3 of the flour and fold into the cake batter. Repeat until all the dry and wet ingredients are over. This should result in 1.5kg of light and ribbony batter.

6. Divide the batter equally into three separate bowls (approximately 500g of batter each). Add in the pink colouring into one bowl and the green colouring into the other bowl and mix well to dye the batters. If you feel the colour is too weak, adjust the colouring per bowl. In the third bowl, fold in the rainbow sprinkles into the batter. Pour each coloured layer into a separate baking tin and bake for 25–30 minutes or until your cake tester comes out clean. Allow to cool completely.

7. For the icing, beat the butter and the icing sugar together until a thick cream is formed, and then add the cream cheese. Place one colour cake at the bottom and apply the icing on top of it, then sandwich another colour cake together with the icing and then cover the top and sides with the icing. Repeat for the third cake as well. Decorate the top of the cake with the reserved rainbow sprinkles.

chocolate biscuit pudding

Serves **6-8** | Prep **40 minutes** | Time **2 hours** | Ethnic Roots **European heritage**

INGREDIENTS

For the pudding:

4 tbsps Dutch processed or high-quality cocoa powder

2 tsps cornflour

100g caster sugar

1 tsp instant coffee

2 egg yolks

360ml milk

50g 70 per cent dark chocolate bar, broken into pieces

1 tsp vanilla extract

2 tsps bourbon (optional)

For the icing:

80g icing sugar

2 tsps cocoa powder

100g butter (room temperature)

For the biscuits:

120ml milk

54 Marie biscuits or rich tea biscuits

CBP is a national treasure. Sri Lankans across the country love this dessert, and everyone will claim to make the best one. This dessert has to be made with Marie or rich tea biscuits—no substitutes!

METHOD

1. Dry-whisk the cocoa powder, the cornflour, sugar and the instant coffee in a pan. Whisk in the egg yolks and the milk. Place the pan over a medium-high heat and continue to whisk for 5 minutes until a smooth chocolate pudding is formed. It will run a bit thinner than usual pudding batter.

2. Take the pudding mixture off the heat. Immediately add in the chocolate pieces, vanilla extract and the bourbon, and mix until all the chocolate is melted. You should be left with a thick pudding mixture. Cover the top of the pudding with cling film to prevent a skin forming on it. Set aside to cool.

3. Beat the icing sugar, cocoa powder and butter together to form a thick batter. Fold the icing into the cooled pudding mixture to give it more structure.

4. Next, take an approximately 9 x 9 inch dish and butter all sides.

5. Pour the milk in a bowl, and one by one, soak a biscuit for around 30 seconds and layer these soft biscuits at the bottom of the buttered dish. Feel free to break some of the biscuits in half, if required, to make a clean first layer. Then add a generous layer of the pudding mixture ensuring that all of the biscuits are covered. Repeat this layering process until you have at least three layers of biscuits and pudding each. Cover with cling film and place in the fridge for a minimum of 2 hours to set and serve. It can be kept in the fridge for 5 days (but it will be devoured much before that)!

the marikkar watalappan

Serves **6-8** | Time **1 hour** | Ethnic Roots **Ceylon Moor**

INGREDIENTS

10 eggs (equivalent to 500g)
500g jaggery, grated
1 tbsp brown or white sugar
360ml thick coconut milk
10 cardamom pods, crushed

Created by the Muslim community, this treasure of a dessert is often served at any big Muslim occasion. My aunts and cousins make the best, best watalappan, and I am honoured to share my Aunty Shifaya and her daughter Minha's beloved recipe with you.

METHOD

1. In a large mixing bowl, beat the 10 eggs by hand with a whisk or a fork, adding the jaggery a little at a time until it is fully dissolved into the egg mixture. It is critical that the custard is not over-beaten and that there are not too many bubbles or air.

2. Add in the sugar, coconut milk, crushed cardamoms and beat into the egg mixture until just combined.

3. Remove the cardamom skins and strain the jaggery custard into a heatproof bowl (preferably metal).

4. Take the heatproof mixing bowl, cover with a lid or foil and steam for 30 minutes until the pudding has set. Serve once cooled.

There is a trick to this recipe: Get good quality jaggery that melts quickly so that you don't end up overwhipping the custard. If you find that your jaggery is not melting into the beaten eggs, then take a small amount of beaten egg and blend it with all the grated jaggery in a blender until a thick custard is formed, then add this back to the beaten eggs and whisk until just combined. And steam the watalappan in a bowl where the circumference of the bottom is much smaller than the top. If you can, steam it in a stainless-steel mixing bowl.

my mum's mango cardamom pudding

Serves **4** | Time **20 minutes** | Ethnic Roots **Multi-Ethnic**

INGREDIENTS

2 very ripe Alphonso mangoes or any other sweet mango, roughly cut into big chunks
200g buffalo curd or Greek yoghurt
50g caster sugar
8 cardamon pods, ground to a powder
1 tbsp lime juice

My mum came up with this fresh, super-easy recipe when I was little. And because she was a busy working mum, she would whip this up as her contribution to any family event. It was so much better than eating fruit cocktail! The trick to getting this recipe perfect is using very ripe mangoes.

METHOD

1. In a food processor, or blender, place all the ingredients except the lime juice and blend till smooth. You should be left with a bright orange yoghurt.

2. Pour into a serving dish, and keep it in the fridge until serving. Just before serving, mix in the lime juice. You can garnish this with your favourite nuts, I love pistachios!

coffee jelly

Serves **4-6** | Prep **20 minutes** | Time **4- 6 hours**

INGREDIENTS

For the jelly:

4 tbsps instant coffee

130g sugar

1 litre hot water

50g gelatine powder

To serve:

200ml milk

2 tsps vanilla extract

2 tsps white sugar

On especially hot days, nothing beats a cold coffee jelly. This is a very simple, yet a very effective dessert. Reach for that jar of instant coffee in the back of the cupboard because it is critical to getting this recipe right!

METHOD

1. In a mixing bowl, dissolve the instant coffee and the sugar in 750ml of hot water. In a measuring jug or a medium bowl, dissolve the gelatine with 250ml of hot water. Add the gelatine solution to the coffee and mix well. Pour the ingredients into a loaf tin or a dish. Cover with clingfilm and allow to set in the fridge for minimum 4 hours.

2. The jelly should be fully set, and you should be able to cut it into cubes. Mix the milk, vanilla extract and sugar together in a small jug. When you serve the coffee jelly in a bowl, pour the milk on top to accompany it; as though it's a deconstructed iced coffee.

sticky date cake

Serves **6-8** | Time **1 hour 30 minutes** | Ethnic Roots **Sinhalese**

INGREDIENTS

For the cake:

1 tsp baking soda

200g dates, pitted

200ml hot water

100g room temperature butter

75g dark brown sugar

3 tbsps kithul treacle syrup

2 eggs

2 tbsps tahini

1 tsp vanilla extract

5g cinnamon stick ground or 1½ tsps cinnamon powder

200g all-purpose flour

2 tsps baking powder

½ tsp fine sea salt

For the toffee sauce:

75g butter, cold and cut into cubes

100g dark brown sugar

3 tbsps of kithul treacle syrup

150ml heavy whipping cream/ double cream

½ tsp sea-salt flakes

Date cake brings memories of Ramadan; they were always the first thing my family members would eat as soon as they broke their fast. I detested dates as a child. And although I still have a love-hate relationship with them, I love me some date cake. One of the most popular cakes that Muslims make during festivals, I have made it that little bit more indulgent.

METHOD

1. Line a square 9 x 9 inch baking pan with parchment paper. Preheat the oven to 180°C.

2. In a bowl, sprinkle the baking soda over the pitted dates, coating them well. Next, soak the dates in hot water for 10 minutes, before grinding the dates and water into a thick paste.

3. In a large bowl, cream the butter, the brown sugar and the kithul syrup with an electric beater until thick and fluffy. Be careful not to overbeat and split the butter, which tends to happen if the butter is cold.

4. Slowly, beat in one egg into the cake batter, ensuring it is fully incorporated before beating in the second. After the eggs are mixed in, beat in the tahini until a smooth batter is formed.

5. Using a spatula, mix in the vanilla extract and cinnamon powder into the batter and fold in the thick date paste. This will ensure you are incorporating air into the mixture and make a light sponge.

6. Sieve in the flour, baking powder and the sea salt into the batter and carefully fold it in until no lumps appear. Pour the batter into a prepared cake tin and bake for 35–40 minutes or until a cake tester comes out clean.

7. Whilst the cake is baking, start on your toffee sauce. Over a medium heat, in a shallow pan, melt the butter, the sugar and the kithul syrup together. Do not stir this, instead swirl the pan to help bring the caramel together. A dark brown caramel will form after 4–5 minutes. Just as all the sugar dissolves, add in the cream and whisk. A thick, dark golden caramel will form. Immediately, take off the heat and add in the sea-salt flakes. Set aside.

8. Once the cake has come out of the oven, you can choose to cool it and transfer it to a cake plate, or if you are like me and lazy, do this in the cake tin. Using a skewer, poke several holes on the top of the cake and pour the caramel over it. Allow it to soak into the cake. Cut and serve with some cream, if you are feeling extra indulgent.

Drinks

'Bomu?' A typical word that comes out of a Sri Lankan's mouth, simply meaning 'Drink?' Lankans love a good cordial and a fruit juice; however, we are not limited to fruits alone. Due to our Ayurvedic practices, we brew many teas and juices to heal the body—coriander tea to fight colds and flu, cumin tea for digestive health, a fenugreek seed water to help with cholesterol— Sri Lankans have a drink for every aliment.

One of the country's iconic exports is our black tea famously known around the world as 'Ceylon Tea'. We have seven different varieties of high-, mid- and low-grown all with their own distinct and unique flavour profiles. I love a good cup of plain or ginger tea, and when I'm on holiday or in a really dull meeting, a good tin kiri tea cannot be beaten.

Some of the serves in this section are a little different in that they are sometimes for one person, sometimes for two. But double the quantities when needed!

faluda

Serves **1** | Time **15 minutes**

INGREDIENTS

1 tsp basil seeds

50ml filtered water

25ml rose syrup

200ml whole milk

METHOD

1. In a glass, mix the water and the basil seeds together and let it sit for 5–10 minutes until the seeds start to moisten.

2. In a highball glass, pour the rose syrup, then add the milk and mix. On the top of the newly made faluda, carefully drain some of the activated seeds and add on the top of the drink. If you have coloured jelly on hand, you can add a few pieces into the drink as well.

iced tea

Serves **4** | Time **1 hour 20 minutes**

INGREDIENTS

20g ground broken orange pekoe black tea

400ml hot water

180ml sugar syrup

80ml lime juice

METHOD

1. In a teapot, brew the black tea with the hot water for 5 minutes. For best results, use filtered water rather than tap. Strain and cool the reserved black tea liquid.

2. In a jug, mix the black tea, the sugar syrup (1:1 ratio of sugar to water) and lime juice together. Garnish with lime slices and serve in highball glasses over lots of ice.

passionfruit gin cocktail

Serves **2 large cocktails** | Time **30 minutes**

INGREDIENTS

400g passionfruit (4 fruits)
250g orange (3 oranges)
10g fresh thyme leaves
100g white sugar
250ml water
100ml good gin

METHOD

1. Scrape the passionfruit pulp into a small stockpot or saucepan. Squeeze the orange juice into the same pan, then add the thyme, sugar and water. Place on high heat and boil for 15 minutes, till you are left with a thick aromatic syrup.

2. Strain the syrup and allow to cool completely.

3. In a short drinking glass, place 3 to 4 ice cubes and then pour 50ml or 100ml (depending how sweet a cocktail you like) of the passionfruit syrup into the glass followed by 50ml of gin. Stir and serve with a wedge of passionfruit as garnish. You could choose to have this as a cordial and simply drink 100ml of syrup topped with soda.

arrack sour

Serves **2 large cocktails** | Time **10 minutes**

INGREDIENTS

50ml good quality arrack
25ml lime juice
1 egg white
25ml sugar syrup (1:1 ratio of sugar to water)

METHOD

1. In a cocktail shaker, add all the ingredients, along with lots of ice. Shake well for at least 3 minutes.

2. Strain and pour into a short drinking glass or a martini glass.

wood apple cream

Serves **4** | Time **10 minutes**

INGREDIENTS

1 large wood apple, broken and pulp reserved

110g grated jaggery

230ml thick coconut milk

400ml water (cold or room temperature)

METHOD

1. Put all the ingredients in a blender and puree until you have a smooth, pulpy light brown juice.

2. Strain through a sieve or chinois into a large jug. Pour into 3–4 glasses to serve.

iced coffee

Serves **2** | Time **25 minutes**

INGREDIENTS

55g ground coffee

250ml hot water

120ml sugar syrup

2 tsps vanilla extract

150ml cold milk

Hazelnut ice cream to serve

METHOD

1. In a cafetière or a coffee pot, brew the ground coffee and the hot water for at least 10 minutes before straining. Reserve the coffee liquid and allow to cool.

2. In a jug, mix the sugar syrup (1:1 ratio of sugar to water), the brewed cooled coffee, vanilla extract and cold milk together. Serve in highball glasses or milkshake glasses with a dollop of hazelnut ice cream (or any flavour you prefer!).

tamarind chilli martini

Serves **4 martini glasses** | Time **15 minutes**

INGREDIENTS

300ml water

150g tamarind pulp, made into a paste

75ml good quality kithul (palm) syrup

1 tsp smoked paprika

25ml lime juice

100ml high quality vodka

METHOD

1. Mix the water and the tamarind together and strain through a chinois.

2. In a cocktail shaker, add plenty of ice, pour in the tamarind paste, the kithul syrup, the paprika, lime juice, vodka and shake well. You know it is well shaken when cold water condensation forms on the outside of the shaker.

3. Strain into martini glasses that have salt and chilli rims and serve.

pineapple margaritas

Serves **4 short glasses** | Time **20 minutes**

INGREDIENTS

Juice of 1 lime

200ml coconut milk

500g fresh pineapple fruit, chopped

2 heaped tsps ginger paste

150ml tequila

METHOD

1. Put all the ingredients in a blender and blend until smooth. Strain and pour into prepared short glasses with a chilli salt rim. Garnish with a piece of pineapple.

kottamali (coriander tea)

Serves **4 teacups** | Time **15 minutes**

INGREDIENTS

75g coriander seeds

30g ginger

3 tsps sugar

METHOD

1. Wash the coriander seeds, drain and set aside. Heat a saucepan over a high heat and dry-roast the washed coriander seeds until they start to change colour and turn dark brown.

2. Immediately add in the water and the ginger, and cook over medium high heat for 5 minutes or until the water resembles a light black tea.

3. Stir in the sugar and boil for another 5 minutes. Strain out the aromatics and serve in teacups.

tin kiri tea

Serves **2 cups** | Time **10 minutes**

INGREDIENTS

4 tbsps condensed milk

3 heaped tsps black loose-leaf tea

4 cloves

2 cardamom pods

½ cinnamon quill

700ml water, room temperature

METHOD

1. Pour the condensed milk into a heatproof mixing jug. In a pestle and mortar, pound the cloves, cardamom and the cinnamon stick together to break it up.

2. In a small pan, mix the loose-leaf tea, the pounded spices and the room temperature water. Put it over a high heat and bring to the boil, approximately 3-5 minutes. You should have a very strong black tea. Strain the tea into the mixing jug with the condensed milk. Mix well until you have a consistency of a milk tea. Serve into two cups and drink hot!

ginger tea

Serves **2 cups** | Time **10 minutes**

INGREDIENTS

3 heaped tsps black loose-leaf tea

30g ginger, lightly pounded

3 tsps sugar

700ml water, room temperature

METHOD

1. In a pestle and mortar, pound the ginger to break it up.

2. In a small pan, mix the loose-leaf tea, the pounded ginger and the room temperature water. Put it over a high heat and bring to the boil, approximately 3-5 minutes. You should have a very strong black tea. Strain the tea into two cups and add 1 ½ tsps of sugar to each one. Stir and serve!

lime and mint cooler

Serves **2 highball glasses** | Time **10 minutes**

INGREDIENTS

450ml water

Juice of two small limes

30g white sugar

30g mint leaves

5 ice cubes

METHOD

1. Put all the ingredients into a blender and blend until all the mint leaves have disintegrated.

2. Strain over ice into a highball glass. Garnish with a lime wedge.

Spicylopedia
know your cupboard essentials

CARDAMOM (ELETTARIA CARDAMOMUM)

A perennial herbaceous plant, cardamom is classified in Ayurveda as one of the rare spices that benefit all three body alignments—fiery, airy and water-dominated. It is mentioned as part of many remedies, food recipes and even as an ingredient of a recreational betel-chewing mix in the twelfth-century Sanskrit text *Manasollasa*.

CHILLI (CAPSICUM ANNUUM)

Brought here by Portuguese traders and later colonialists, both chilli and Sri Lanka adapted exceptionally well to one another. There's even a local idiom that immortalizes this historic encounter with chilli: 'ingurudilamirisgattawagei', which compares Sri Lankans exchanging the gentler spiciness of ginger with the red-hot taste of chilli to the King's tricky alliance with the Dutch colonists to dispel the Portuguese. Well-suited to Sri Lanka's climate, chilli spread throughout the island and over time, welcomed several varieties from the everyday green chilli to the notoriously tear-jerking nai-miris.

CINNAMON (CINNAMOMUM VERUM)

One of the staple condiments used in Sri Lankan cooking is the unrivalled Ceylon cinnamon. Aromatic, pungent and astringent, cinnamon comes from the bark of an evergreen tree that grows up to thirty feet uncultivated, and about twelve feet cultivated. According to Ayurveda, cinnamon is detoxifying, energizing and has pain-alleviation abilities, making it a common ingredient in home remedies for colds, congestion and arthritic pains.

CLOVES (SYZYGIUMAROMATICUM)

Picked as unopened buds and sundried until they become deep brown in colour, the yellow-white clove flowers rarely see the sun. Cloves have a distinct flavour and the Sri Lankan yellow rice is not be complete without it. Ayurveda classes it as a condiment with a 'cold' potency. Cloves are the undisputed Lankan remedy for any oral or dental disease, whether it's a toothache, bleeding gums or bad breath.

COCONUT (COCOS NUCIFERA)

Coconut forms the base of most curries, certain rice dishes, desserts, drinks and even medicines in Sri Lanka. In Sri Lankan markets you can buy fresh, husked coconuts that require some skill and practice to break, or you can opt for dried packaged flakes or powder. Sri Lanka has several coconut cultivars used for different purposes, such as drinking coconut water, cooking, oil extraction, making the alcoholic beverage arrack and even for sport (pora pol is a variety with canonball-like hard fruits used for 'coconut fighting'). In Lankan cooking, coconut is often used in grated flake form or as coconut milk, which is extracted by squeezing its flesh.

CORIANDER SEED AND LEAVES (CORIANDRUM SATIVUM)

Coriander or cilantro is a herb with some incredible healing properties and is used in almost all home remedies for colds and fever, including the Sri Lankan classic inguru-kottamalli (ginger-coriander brew). Local healers use it for treating swellings, asthma, nausea, gastritis, body pains and even urinary tract infections. In our culinary culture, coriander has a special place as one of the three essential ingredients of the Sri Lankan curry powder mix 'tuna-paha' which means 'three or five'. Mentions of cilantro leaves in traditional Sri Lankan recipes are quite rare—almost absent. From what I've discovered, use of cilantro in its leaf form came about recently due to the cross-pollination between local and foreign recipes served in urban restaurants, and the growing influence of local chefs who have studied or worked abroad, or are simply inspired by exotic culinary practices.

CUMIN (CUMINUM CYMINUM)

Cumin is an elongated brown seed of an annual herbaceous plant. It completes the Sri Lankan curry powder trinity, so this should establish just how important cumin is to the Lankan food culture. It's present in all forms of foods, from curries, rice and street food to sweets. Ayurveda classifies cumin as a condiment with 'hot potency', and it holds a special place as a digestive aid in the local foodlore.

CURRY LEAVES (MURRAYAKOENIGII)

There's a proverb among Sri Lankan Tamils and the Sinhalese that roughly translates to 'you can't sneak out the curry leaves'. It refers to small matters that are difficult to hide, just as curry leaves are impossible to sneak out unnoticed from your neighbour's yard due to their unmissable aroma. Some Sri Lankans believe that curry leaves absorb toxins and impurities in food, which explains the common practice of leaving them uneaten in a small pile in a corner of your plate. Another belief is that they should be eaten with the meal, as curry leaves are a powerful digestive aid—a claim well-supported by Ayurvedic texts.

FENNEL SEED (FOENICULUM VULGARE)

With a subtle but distinct flavour built on sweet, pungent and bitter tastes, fennel or sweet cumin brings in an interesting hint of mild licorice-like relish. Fennel seeds come from a hardy, edible perennial flowering plant and it's one of the spices that go into making curry powder, one of the staples of the Lankan culinary tradition. Fennel always takes me back to a popular children's treat in the subcontinent: a single seed is covered in a smooth layer of hyper-coloured sugar icing called 'hoonubittara' in Sinhala (meaning 'gecko eggs'), which is a pretty accurate comparison considering their shape and size.

FENUGREEK SEEDS (ANETHUM GRAVEOLENS)

Fenugreek brings in a sweet, hot aroma and a light bitter taste that adds an interesting depth to food. Within traditional recipes, it is often mentioned for pickles, as an additive that enriches curry powder flavours and as a binding agent that thickens curries up. Fenugreek belongs to the pea family, and grows as an annual plant going up to about 1 1/2 half feet. Cultivated for its nutrition-heavy leaves and seeds, Ayurvedic healers use it to control diabetes, eczema, menstrual disorders, haemorrhoids and also to stimulate lactation in breastfeeding women. New research shows that fenugreek can actually play a role in lowering serum cholesterol and controlling blood sugar levels in diabetic patients.

GORAKA/ GAMBOGE (GARCINIA ZEYLANICA, GARCINIA QUAESITA, GARCINIA XANTHOCHYMUS)

Goraka, brindleberry, Malabar tamarind, kodukkaippuli, kudampuli, are some names used to describe one of Sri Lanka's most interesting, intensely sour condiments. There are three varieties common in the local cuisine—rath (red), kaha (yellow) and rata (foreign). Goraka grows naturally, reaching as high as 65 feet. Perhaps it is the dark leaves casting a thick shade, and the tree shedding old branches with loud crashes that inspired myths about demons residing in gorakas. When goraka started gaining international popularity as a fat-busting superfood, the government tried to persuade more Sri Lankans to grow it. But the legends involving demonic spirits proved to be hard to shake off, even with the promise of money.

LEMONGRASS (CYMBOPOGON CITRATUS)

Lemongrass brings a light citrus taste and aroma much milder than lime itself. There are so many species of lemongrass that there's usually some confusion about the culinary variety. In Sri Lanka, it's the citratus species (West Indian Lemongrass). Traditionally, lemongrass was also used as a medicinal herb against colds and congestion, an organic agricultural pesticide and as a food preservative with fantastic antifungal properties.

MINT LEAVES (MENTA PIPERITA)

You are most likely to come across mint in Sri Lankan food as a garnish, sauce or sambol. Mentha is a plant genus that carries the active ingredient menthol, it has several edible mint species and out of these, peppermint, also known as curled mint, is the variety used most often in Lankan foods. A herbaceous perennial plant, peppermint is a hybrid of water mint and spearmint. Peppermint can usually be encountered as a home remedy for congestion and as an ingredient in headache balms that many Sri Lankans carry with them to avoid tropical heat migraines.

MUSTARD SEEDS (BRASSICA JUNCEA)

This delicious spice has been part of Sri Lankans' lives—think of the practice of referring to mustard seeds when describing minuscule things. The brown mustard variety traditionally used in our food comes from a perennial herb, growing up to a metre or so, with bright yellow, little flowers. Ayurvedic texts classify mustard as a condiment with 'hot' potency and prescribe it for lung infections and thyroid diseases. Mustard is used in Lankan foods whole, powdered or finely ground, to bring in that signature 'earthy-bitter' tone.

NUTMEG (MYRISTICA FRAGRANS)

The nutmeg fruit ripens to open up and reveal a stunningly crimson, vein-like lacy skin covering the single, deep brown seed. Both this seed and the dried skin—called mace—are used as spices. They have a warm, slightly sweet taste that is perfect for baking and desserts. Thought to have originated in Indonesia, nutmeg is a tropical evergreen tree that grows very tall, sometimes even up to 65 feet. Lankan folklore lists nutmeg among the auspicious plants to grow at one's home. Home remedies for nausea, vomiting and particularly, stomachaches prescribe nutmeg. It's also part of the betel-chewing kit traditionally gifted to monks and the elderly.

PANDAN LEAVES/ RAMPE (PANDANASAMARYLLIFOLIUS)

Pandan carries a savoury-sweet flavour that comes paired with a very distinct fragrance. This 'rampe' smell has become the trademark aroma that many Sri Lankans associate with the perfect rice and this is also why they are included in recipes for local desserts, sticky rice-based puddings and custards. Pandan leaves are flat, smooth, long blades with sharp edges. They grow in fan-shaped clusters on a tropical tree type. In Lankan herb-lore, pandan leaves are mentioned in remedies for vomiting, headaches, flatulence and dyspepsia.

Index

Acknowledgements

Special thanks to Aarthi Dharmadasa, Afdhel Aziz, Amarilli Edwards, Anjeli Rajeswari, Anushka Wijesinha, Asvajit Boyle, Azam Latiff, Cinnamon Grand Hotel, Dentsu Grant Group Sri Lanka, Farhana Marikkar, Felix Buxton, Hemu Ramiah, Joss Yerbury, Lee Bazalgette, Louise Rae Perry, Minha Akram, Mumtaz Nastar, Shamalee De Silva Parizeau, and Sebastian Posingis. You have provided me advice, support and kindness at every stage of this book process. Thank you for contributing to this labour of love.

About the Author

TASHA MARIKKAR is a writer, marketer, music festival curator, amateur illustrator and an unofficial food tourism ambassador for Sri Lanka. Born and bred Sri Lankan, Tasha grew up in Colombo during the height of the conflict. She describes herself as a real 'achcharu', meaning that her ethnic background is mixed—Colombo Chetty, Sinhalese and Ceylon Moor. This has given her a unique perspective on her homeland.

Tasha's family was entrenched in the advertising business in Sri Lanka and this is where her passion for food brands began. She spent countless hours cooking and developing recipes at home; however, her education took her to London to pursue her degree at the London School of Economics and Political Science. This is where she has lived since 2004.

In 2010, Tasha and her sister co-founded the Electric Peacock Festival in Sri Lanka, bringing in Grammy Award-winning artists like Roger Sanchez, Basement Jaxx and Mark Ronson to headline the music event. After working in London for over ten years in advertising, Tasha took a break to write this, her first cookbook. She now spends her time developing recipes, cooking pop-ups across the world and has a greater vision to tackle and create solutions to fight hunger in Sri Lanka.

To know more, visit:

www.jayaflava.com

www.tashamarikkar.con

Instagram—@jayaflava

![HarperCollins logo] **HarperCollins** *Publishers* India

At HarperCollins India, we believe in telling the best stories and finding the widest readership for our books in every format possible. We started publishing in 1992; a great deal has changed since then, but what has remained constant is the passion with which our authors write their books, the love with which readers receive them, and the sheer joy and excitement that we as publishers feel in being a part of the publishing process.

Over the years, we've had the pleasure of publishing some of the finest writing from the subcontinent and around the world, including several award-winning titles and some of the biggest bestsellers in India's publishing history. But nothing has meant more to us than the fact that millions of people have read the books we published, and that somewhere, a book of ours might have made a difference.

As we look to the future, we go back to that one word— a word which has been a driving force for us all these years.

Read.